W9-CTN-539

Butterflies of the North Woods

YMCA CAMP WIDJIWAGAN
3788 NORTH ARM RD
ELY, MN 55731

TO WIDJI STAFF

THANKS FOR ALL
YOUR HELP!!

Butterflies
of the North Woods
By Larry Weber

[signature]

Kollath-Stensaas
PUBLISHING

Kollath-Stensaas Publishing
394 Lake Avenue South, Suite 406
Duluth, MN 55802
(218) 727-1731

BUTTERFLIES *of the* NORTH WOODS

©2001 by Mark Stensaas, Rick Kollath and Larry Weber. All rights
reserved. Except for short excerpts for review purposes, no part of this
book may be reproduced or transmitted in any form by any means,
electronic or mechanical, including photocopying, without permission in
writing from the publisher.

Printed in Korea by Doosan Corporation
10 9 8 7 6 5 4 3 2 1   First Edition

Editorial Director: Mark Sparky Stensaas
Graphic Designer: Rick Kollath

ISBN 0-9673793-1-8

Table of Contents

To Fran,

My companion in many
butterfly counts and the one
who shares the joys of
watching nearby-nature
throughout the year.

Acknowledgements

Writing *Butterflies of the North Woods* has been an exciting and rewarding project for me. Like all publications, there are many who have helped in a variety of ways to make this project a reality.

John Weber patiently helped me identify some of the butterflies that I photographed. Dave Benson, Judy Gibbs, Retta James-Gasser and Dale Kane all invited me to speak about butterflies and show my slides at their events. It was at one such presentation that Mark Sparky Stensaas approached me about writing a local guide book. His excitement and encouragement helped us formulate the ideas and format of the book.

My students also deserve mention for showing the energy and curiosity of their age. They often tell me about the "black-and-orange" butterflies they find in the spring and white and yellow ones in the fall.

And of course, my wife Fran who patiently answered my computer questions and proofread much of the manuscript. As always, she has been a delightful and observant companion in many of our local butterfly counts.

To everyone; Thanks!

Larry Weber

March 10, 2001

Kollath-Stensaas Publishers wish to thank Larry for his full involvement in this major undertaking. His breadth of knowledge of the natural world is legendary.

Thanks to Dave Benson and Connie Stensaas for proofreading the manuscript and finding those little mistakes that had eluded us.

Susan Gustafson also gave us help that no one else could have given.

Though we mainly used Larry's splendid photographs, we filled in the gaps with images from Rod Planck, Ann Swengel and Jeffrey Glassberg; all fine naturalists in their own right.

Finally, a big thanks to Jeffrey Glassberg and the North American Butterfly Association who proofread the text and made sure all our butterfly facts were accurate and all the names were compatible with the NABA checklist. We are proud that this book is a NABA-approved field guide.

The Publishers; Mark Sparky Stensaas, Rick Kollath

April 16, 2001

Parts of the Butterfly

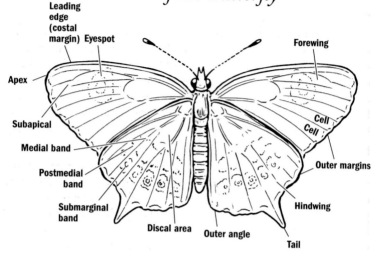

Leading edge (costal margin)
Eyespot
Forewing
Apex
Cell
Cell
Subapical
Medial band
Postmedial band
Outer margins
Submarginal band
Hindwing
Discal area
Outer angle
Tail

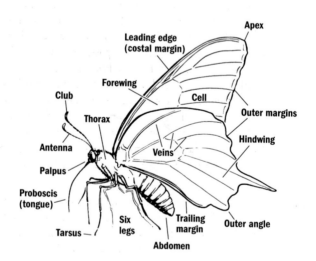

Apex
Leading edge (costal margin)
Forewing
Club
Cell
Thorax
Outer margins
Antenna
Hindwing
Palpus
Veins
Proboscis (tongue)
Trailing margin
Six legs
Outer angle
Tarsus
Abdomen

Parts of the Caterpillar

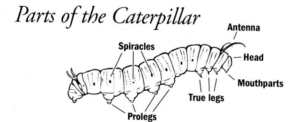

Antenna
Spiracles
Head
Mouthparts
True legs
Prolegs

What is a Butterfly?

What is a Butterfly?

Butterflies are insects that enjoy a position of love and acceptance in our culture not allowed many of their kind. We eagerly invite them into our yards–unlike most other bugs–probably because they are beautifully-colored and often associated with flowers. Photogenic and graceful, they are the picture of freedom. We see them as non-threatening since none bite or are poisonous. At a time when we desire to learn more about near-by nature, butterflies stand out as wild critters we can all know and enjoy.

Butterfly Body Parts

Like other insects, butterflies have three body segments: **head**, **thorax** and **abdomen** with a chitinous **exoskeleton**. On the head, they have large compound eyes, club-shaped **antennae**, a pair of furry **palpi** (mouth-parts), and a long coiled tube for a mouth. This **proboscis** is a tongue and is used to take in fluids. Most butterflies feed the on nectar of flowers, but some take in sap, fruit juices, carrion, dung or moisture from wet soils.

The **thorax** is where the legs and wings are attached. All butterflies do have six legs though some species have small and nearly useless front legs. The lower portion of the leg is called the **tarsus**. On it is located smell receptors for identifying food and plants to deposit eggs on. It is the exposed four wings that give identity to these beautiful insects.

The long and thin **abdomen** may be the only body part that in any way resembles their immature stage–the caterpillars. Here are found internal organs of digestion, respiration, circulation and reproduction. Small holes called **spiracles** aid in respiration and line the abdomen's sides. On the tail end of the male are **claspers** for grasping the female during mating. Females have an **ovipositor** for egg laying at abdomen's end.

Lepidoptera

Butterflies belong to the order of Lepidoptera. *Lepido* refers to scales and *ptera* means wings. Wings of the butterflies are covered by overlapping small flat growths, called **scales**, that often rub off like dust. Both the butterflies and their cousins, the moths, have such wings.

Of the 120,000 known species of Lepidoptera worldwide, 95 percent are moths! About 700 kinds of butterflies can be found in North America. The North Woods of Minnesota, Wisconsin and Michigan are home to over 120 species with 60 of these being more common.

Butterflies can be distinguished from moths in several ways. Butterflies are dayflying with clubbed antennae and colorful wings that are held over the back during rest...generally. Most moths are nocturnal with feathery antennae and drab wings held flat at rest...usually. There are exceptions to all these traits. Moths have a coupling mechanism, the **frenulum**, that attaches the wings. Butterflies lack this. Though not often seen, its presence may be the most sure feature for distinguishing moths.

Butterfly wings are large, colorful and veined. Composed of many sections called cells, they are the most noticed part of these insects. Wings allow butterflies to take flight, but also function in courtship, camouflage and body temperature regulation. Patterns and other features are often species-specific and can be quick, identifying field marks. Males may have specialized scales called **androconia** or **stigma**, that give off sexual-attraction scents or **pheromones**. **Sexual dimorphism**, where males and females of the same species look different, often exists among butterflies, but not as dramatically as with birds. Males may be slightly brighter, larger or show different colors or patterns.

Areas and margins of wings have diagnostic names. Terms can get lengthy and complicated, but only a few are needed to understand their features. Front or **forewings** tend to be smaller and more triangular than the back or **hindwings**. The **leading edge** or front margin is called **costal** while the rear edge margin is referred to as the outer or **trailing edge**. The front wing tip is the **apex**. Areas of the wing are described as **basal** (near body), **medial** (middle), **submarginal** (just in from the outer edge) or **marginal** (near the outer edge). Individual areas between the veins are known as **cells**.

Wing colors are seldom plain. Color patterns can be bands, stripes, rows, dots, blotches or eyespots. Eyespots have nothing to do with true eyes, but when seen on wings, they often resemble them. Between and behind these various patterns, wing scales are in shades from white to blue to brown to yellow or orange.

In the tropics, butterflies are much bigger than in our part of the country. Some may have wingspans larger than a hand. Though different measurements are done for the various butterflies, most wingspans are determined as the breadth of the open wings. Some butterflies such as skippers and blues seldom sit in this position, but the same measurements are used. Therefore, the actual specimen may look smaller than the given wingspan.

Behavior of the "Flutter-Bys"

Butterflies do more than just flutter by. With a little patience and perseverance one can interpret what butterflies are doing and why. Easily observed behaviors include courtship, mating, territorial defense, feeding, basking, puddling and hilltopping. Sit quietly in a preferred butterfly spot on a warm sunny day. Use your binoculars. Take notes. And enjoy the show.

Mature butterflies are usually **territorial** and males spend much of their days flying back and forth within this zone of home turf. They appear to be driving away other males or courting any females that pass by. Aggressive species will even chase away much larger butterflies of other species.

Unmated butterflies, especially males, can frequently be seen at damp sand or mud puddles where they ingest minerals and water. This behavior is called **puddling**. Social rites may exist here at these local watering holes (sometimes referred to as "singles bars"...well, they are unmated males at the "sand bar".) Tiger Swallowtails are notorious puddlers.

Above. Tiger Swallowtails "puddling" at a wet riverbank. These males are taking up minerals and water.

Below. Hundreds of European Skippers gather on a wet gravel road. Puddling behavior is easily observed.

Hilltopping refers to butterfly congregations at open sites on steep hillsides or hilltops. Males again outnumber females at these locations, as they patrol and search for females.

Mated females are likely to be found elsewhere, mostly in meadows, fields or swamps. Here they search for host plants to lay eggs on. Using smell receptors on their antennae and leg tarsi, they are able to recognize the appropriate plants. Their preferred habitats are vital to their lives and the continued success of the species. **Egg laying** is a difficult behavior to observe but being in the right place (in a patch of their favorite host plant) at the right time can help.

Adult butterflies feed primarily on flower nectar. Such diets may be specific to one group of flowers or general, depending on the kind of butterfly. **Nectaring** is probably the easiest behavior to observe. A few do not nec-

The Commas get their sugar fix not from flower nectar but from tree sap and rotting fruit.

tar at all and only take tree sap, rotting fruit juices, water or minerals with their coiled proboscis. Some butterfly species will feed on bird guano or sweat-stained clothes. In these cases they are taking in salts and other minerals that they need.

Body temperature greatly depends on air temperature. Butterfly bodies need to reach a relatively warm temperature in order to flap their wings with

V-shaped tears out of the wings indicate an unsuccessful attack by a bird. The Mourning Cloak (lower photo) appears to have survived several attacks.

Basking with open wings allows this Mourning Cloak to soak up the warmth of the sun.

enough energy to fly. Warming up is done by **basking**. Some spread their wings in sunny sites and act like small solar panels to collect heat. Others are lateral baskers. These butterflies will sit perpendicular to the sun with wings closed soaking up the sun's warmth. Basking is a very common and easily observed behavior.

Wings do wear and fade over time as they lose many of the shingled scales that they emerged with. V-shaped tears out of their wings reflect the near miss of a bird predator. Of course, many don't escape the birds, mammals, insects or spiders that feed on these colorful insects.

Mating in butterflies is not a face-to-face experience. It is facilitated by the male's claspers. These are Hairstreaks.

Here a comma is taking up salts through its proboscis from a sweat-stained hat. Butterflies seek out the minerals they need wherever they can find them.

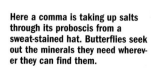

Butterfly Biology 101

Monarch eggs on a common milkweed leaf.

Two small Monarch larvae (caterpillars) fatten up on milkweed.

Pupation is not far away when the caterpillar reaches this size.

Butterflies go through amazing changes in their developmental journey. Such a life cycle, called **complete metamorphosis**, has four distinct stages. Eggs hatch to become **larvae** (caterpillars) which transform into **pupae** (chrysalises) and emerge as the winged adults we know and love.

In the North Woods, where we have four distinct seasons, each species needs to deal with both the heat and cold. All butterflies will survive the winter in one form or another. Some do so as eggs, some as caterpillars, others as pupae and still others as adults. Only the monarch is truly migratory while a few others head south on a partial migration.

After mating, females seek specific plants where they lay eggs. Sensors on the feet help her identify the exact host species. Eggs are laid singly or in clusters of a few to several hundred. Shapes and features vary from species to species. Eggs may be round, cone-shaped, flat, smooth or ribbed.

Caterpillars have simple eyes, chewing jaws, three pair of jointed legs near the front and five pair of grasping prolegs near the rear. **Prolegs** look like real legs but technically are not. Food for the fast-growing larvae is the leaves of the plants on which the eggs were laid. Caterpillars feed constantly and grow quickly. They molt each time they reach a larger phase. The final molt produces the chrysalis.

Unlike moth cocoons, the butterfly **chrysalis** is composed of a translucent skin. Though it may be protected by an overhanging leaf, the chrysalis lacks the camouflaging coverings of the cocoon. Many butterflies hang the chrysalis by the "tail" at a site called the **cremaster**. Others stand upright and our held in place by a "safety belt" of silk.

Adults often emerge in ten days to two weeks, or in some species, not until next spring. When emerging from a spilt in the chrysalis skin, they pull their bodies out and pump fluids into the veins of the folded wings. Shortly, the colorful adult emerges. After some drying and adjusting of their body temperature, they fly off.

Almost as soon as the adult butterfly can fly, they begin courting. This may involve dancing flights or wing stroking. Mating often lasts several hours and usually happens in flight. Males use claspers to hold the female, but he does not always lift her.

Adulthood lasts about two weeks though it can stretch to as long as eight months in hiber-

The Monarch chrysalis is flecked with gold. It hangs by a structure called the cremaster.

After emerging, fluids are pumped through the veins of the crumpled wings.

nating species. Generations are called broods. Northern species are usually single brooded but some species have up to three broods per year. In the North Woods only the American Coppers, Cabbage Whites, Eastern Tailed-Blues, American Ladies, Clouded and Orange Sulphurs are regularly triple-brooded.

Above. With wings now fully dry and fluid-filled, the Monarch gets ready to fly.

Left. Mating starts the Monarch's life cycle all over again.

Butterfly Observation

For many years learning about butterflies meant collecting. The normal procedure of learning about them was to net, kill and pin the specimen. Though such collections have taught us much about butterflies, modern optics now allow us to view and observe these interesting critters without disturbing them.

Serious butterfly observation, or "butterflying", demands the use of binoculars, especially the close-focus type. Ones that do not focus clearly from a distance of less than ten feet will cause you to step back and you will not get as close a view as is sometimes needed for identification. Binocular technology has come a long way in the last few years and there are many quality optics out there. Compact binoculars are often harder to hold steady than full-size optics, but are easily packed on a hike. See Appendix F for a list of good butterflying binoculars.

Similar things can be said for close-up photography. The idea is to get close enough to fill the frame with the butterfly. Thirty-five millimeter SLR cameras with macro lenses or zoom lenses combined with close-up filters provide excellent photos for nearly anyone trying this setup. For detailed photographic technique see Larry West's *How to Photograph Insects and Spiders* or John Shaw's *Closeups in Nature.* (see Appendix E). Using your own pictures taken in nearby yards, fields or parks is a great way to learn the kinds of local butterflies. Butterfly guides of yore featured only dead museum specimens pinned flat out. Now, this guide, and others listed in the Titles of Interest appendix, rely on actual field photos of free-flying butterflies.

Flight times are indicated by the red-bar phenograms under each species photo. Phenograms show the time of year when the adults are on the wing though butterflies do survive the entire year in one form or another. Peak flight times usually last a month or more and coincide with the blooming of favorite nectar flowers. These host plants are well enough developed at this time to also sustain the eggs and caterpillars. Anyone studying the local butterflies also becomes a student of the native flora.

But, by all means, the best way to observe butterflies is to patiently watch as they nectar, court or bask at regularly used sites. Butterflies in the north tend to be most active on sunny calm days between 10 a.m. and 5 p.m. The extremely early or late hours often associated with wildlife watching need not be kept when one is butterflying. Enjoy them even if you see only a few species. They are magnificent and impressive insects. Many a life-long naturalist has begun by watching backyard butterflies.

Identification

At first, many butterflies can look similar. As with birding, good identification skills take time to develop. A number of features help to separate the different species. Size, usually measured by wingspan, is one of
the most obvious characteristics. Swallowtails and monarchs are considered large butterflies while the skippers, blues, crescents and coppers
would be considered small. Most are middle-sized with wingspans of one-
and-a-half to two-and-a-half inches.

Color is an easy feature to observe whether on the forewing or hindwing, above or below. All butterflies have field marks that help us deter-
mine their identity. Stripes, dots, "tails", eyespots, margin lines and camouflage patterns are all features used to key out species. Seeing these
markings requires both patience and good optics. Do not try to learn to
identify butterflies in a hurry. Sketching or note-taking of the butterfly's
appearance and behavior can also help. Comparing your journal notes to
the identification tips and photos in this book will be a great help in butterfly recognition.

Fritillaries, blues and skippers may be quite challenging and field identification requires much practice. Continuous observation allows one to
quickly pick out the important field marks. Even when we cannot deter-
mine the species, just watching these insects is an interesting and rewarding experience.

Fourth of July Butterfly Count

The North American Butterfly Association uses the month of July to con-
duct population and species counts. Known as the Fourth of July
Butterfly Count, the parameters are similar to those of the Christmas Bird
Count conducted by the National Audubon Society each winter. Spotters
count the kinds and number of butterflies seen within a fifteen mile
diameter circle. All counting happens on a single day; preferably a clear,
calm and warm day, between 10 a.m. and 5 p.m. Each year more and
more amateur naturalists are participating in an ever-increasing number
of counts. This trend will continue as butterflies get better known and
butterflying becomes more accepted as a life-long hobby.

How to use this Field Guide

Butterflies of the North Woods is designed to make field identification easier for you, the reader. Through the use of color photos, arrows pointing to field marks, size scales, phenograms and habitats, we have made a handy, compact and easy to use guide. Also by limiting the butterflies to those found in one geographic area we have eliminated the need to wade through hundreds of species, many of which would never be found in the North Woods. The Phenology Flight Chart (Appendix C.) will aid in knowing when to be in the field and the Favorite Food List (Appendix D.) will tell you what flowers to look for while out and about.

For the purposes of this book we will define the North Woods as the area underlain by the granite of the Canadian Shield. This would encompass northeast Minnesota, northern Wisconsin, the Upper Peninsula of Michigan, parts of Ontario, Quebec and New England. This book focuses on Minnesota, Wisconsin and Michigan. But remember, not all species are found in any single area. Habitat preferences tend to spread these species out. The North Woods is a mosaic of habitats from pine barrens to meadows to bogs to suburban yards. Tree cover varies from cut over aspen to pine plantation to northern hardwood forest. Check out the Habitat Guide in Appendix B.

Order

Butterflies are organized by families and then broken down further into subfamily. In this book we list species according to the North American Butterfly Association (NABA) checklist. Family name is listed at the bottom of the left page of each species-spread while the subfamily is listed on the bottom of the right page. With experience in the field using this guide, you will gradually learn to identify butterflies to family. This is especially important for the small confusing butterflies such as the skippers. It is for this reason that we have chosen not to arrange by color. In the long run it is better to learn butterfly families.

Butterfly Names

Like other organisms, butterflies are given both common and scientific names. The common names are the English names most amateur naturalists use, while the scientific or Latin names tend to be the spoken word of entomologists and lepidopterists. Unfortunately, butterfly names have been in a state of flux for quite some time. In 1995, the North American Butterfly Association (NABA) published a checklist of butterfly names. This has been a step towards standardization and has been adopted by many authors. We use the NABA names in this book. In a few situations, the subspecies (a third Latin name) is used. This is done only if there is enough variation in the subspecies to make it appear different from the parent species.

Photos

We chose to use photos of free-flying butterflies in their natural habitat. Most photos are by the author and taken in northern Minnesota and Wisconsin. (Photo credits are listed on page 168.) Attempting to illustrate both the underwing and above-wing patterns of each species, we show both a folded-wing and a spreadwing, or basking photo. If their common resting position is spreadwing, that is what we illustrate first.

The red phenogram indicates when you are most likely to see that butterfly on the wing.

Black size-bar shows average wingspan length for that species.

Photos on the right side of the spread highlight different life stages, other resting postures, sexual dimorphism and/or unique behaviors.

Nature Notes are natural history tidbits about that species. *Larry's Phenology Records* **are actual emergence dates taken from the author's extensive field notes.**

Habitats that the butterfly frequents are listed here.

Family name is listed on the lower left hand page and subfamily is found on the right page.

Fieldmark Arrows

Arrows point to diagnostic features in the photos which are referenced in the description text and marked with an arrow symbol (↑). These are characteristics that you should look for while in the field. Jotting down notes on bands, eyespots, colors and other wing marks will help you identify the butterfly when you have a chance to consult this book.

Size Scale

Size is relative and often hard to judge in the field. Use the life-size silhouettes at the beginning of each family section to familiarize yourself with average sizes of different groups. Also at the top of each species' main photo is a black bar that indicates the length of the average wingspan for that species.

Phenograms

What is a phenogram? All butterflies live out their lives according to seasonal timing that is characteristic and consistent for that species. Our phenogram highlights in red the time when that species is active as a flying and feeding adult. In other words, look for that butterfly during the highlighted weeks/months. This can also help narrow down your identification search. Let's say you see a dark, medium-sized butterfly in April. By field characteristics you think it could have been either a Mourning Cloak or a Black Swallowtail. Noting the phenograms for each, you conclude that it most likely was a Mourning Cloak since Black Swallowtails do not emerge until June.

Habitat

Preferred habitat is found beneath the phenogram. These are the places where that particular species can most likely be found–but not exclusively. Butterflies have wings and can move quickly from area to area. That is why we list several favored habitats. Species that are strongly linked to a specific biome and live out most of their life cycle there, have only one habitat listed. An example would be the Bog Coppers which rarely stray from the confines of the acid bog.

Nature Notes

Nature Notes are fascinating bits of natural history that bring one a more complete understanding of that species. Unique behavior, population trends, naming history and flight characteristics are just some of the topics touched on.

Sidebars

Occasionally quotes are taken from the author's first book, *Backyard Almanac* and placed as a sidebar. **Larry's Phenology Records** is a sidebar for some species that highlights actual northern Minnesota spring emergence dates from the author's extensive field notes.

Species Text

Description covers the wing pattern, both above and below, of adult butterflies. If males and females are different (sexual dimorphism) then these differences are described. Measurements given are the wingspan of a butterfly when wings are held open and flat. Most species rest with spread wings but some butterflies such as the blues and skippers often rest with wings held vertical over the back. Remember this as you use these measurements.

Under **Similar Species**, other butterflies that could be confused with that species are described and differences highlighted.

Life Cycle speaks to the number of broods that that butterfly can have in our area in one season. A brood is one generation of egg laying. Flight period is also listed.

Eggs, **Caterpillar** and **Chrysalis** describe their respective categories. Butterfly caterpillars are often duller, smaller and less distinct than most moth caterpillars. Because of this, we have chosen not to illustrate the caterpillars for the majority of species.

Wintering refers to the state in which that species spends the winter. The options for surviving the bitter cold of winter are several; butterflies can overwinter as a hibernating adult, in egg form, as a caterpillar or chrysalis, or migrate to more temperate climes. Only the Monarch is a long-distance migrant in our area.

Caterpillar Food and **Adult Food** are the last categories. Food for adult butterflies is usually flower nectar, fruit or sap. Caterpillars eat leaves. Listed are the preferred species found in our area. To increase your chances of finding a certain butterfly in the field, go out on a sunny, calm day in an area where their favorite adult food is in bloom.

Day-flying Moths: Butterfly Imposters

There are several moths in our area that don't behave like moths. They are day-flying and some have butterfly-like antennae. This two-page spread starting on page 150 highlights three butterfly imposters.

Glossary

We have tried not to use technical jargon in the text. Check out page 152 for the easy-to-understand meanings of some tricky terms.

North Woods Butterfly Checklist

In Appendix A you will find a checklist of all 120-plus species regularly found in the North Woods of Minnesota, Wisconsin and Michigan. Check off the ones you see in your travels afield. For identifying butterflies not found in this book we recommend Jeffrey Glassberg's *Butterflies*

Through Binoculars by Oxford University Press (1999). This comprehensive guide covers all the species found in the eastern U.S.

Habitat Guide

Appendix B groups some common butterflies as to their preferred North Woods habitat. You may not always find them there, but it is the best place to start looking for them.

Phenology Flight Chart

An extremely useful Phenology Flight Chart is shown in Appendix C This chart illustrates the flight times for some common butterflies, starting with the earliest and continuing through to the late-season flyers. At a glance one can easily see which species would be likely during that time period.

Favorite Food List

Certain butterfly species like to feed on certain flowers. In Appendix D we have listed the favorite nectar flowers found in the North Woods. Photographs of the most important plants are included. You can bet that when one of these plants is in bloom, you will find butterflies.

Titles of Interest

This list of recommended reading and resources includes our favorite titles for delving deeper into the fascinating world of the "flutter-bys". Also listed are books on close-up nature photography. Appendix E.

Binoculars for Butterflying

Recommended binoculars are those that focus close and are of good quality. Check out Appendix F if you are in the market for new "glass".

Butterfly Conservation Groups

Butterfly clubs and organizations are a great way to meet others with similar interests. Contact these folks for membership information. Appendix G.

Enjoy *Butterflies of the North Woods*. Take it in the field. Cram it in your pack. Use it. But most importantly, have fun getting to know our fascinating northern butterflies.

Canadian Tiger Swallowtail

Swallowtails
Family Papilionidae

The majority of this family is found in the tropics with about 600 species worldwide. About thirty can be found in North America. Most are large and colorful, often with "tails" on the hind wings. They have six walking legs and use the long proboscis for taking nectar.

Eggs are globular and placed on host plants. Immature caterpillars resemble bird droppings and feed at night. When fully grown, many of the caterpillars have eyespots on the thorax and fleshy horns (osmeteria) behind the head. Chrysalises are green or brown with a silken girdle around the middle. All members of the Swallowtail family overwinter as a chrysalis.

Swallowtails (Subfamily Papilioninae)

Black Swallowtail *Papilio polyxenes*

MAY	JUNE	JULY	AUGUST	SEPTEMBER

Open areas, old fields, meadows, lawns, parks, vacant lots, farmlands, stream banks.

Nature Notes:

Tend to stay closer to the ground than other swallowtails.

The caterpillars mimic bird droppings.

Description: Wingspan is 3½ to 4½ inches.

Above: Male is black to blue-black with yellow spots that form two bands across all wings Border with yellow spots and chevrons. Hindwing reveals an orange eyespot with black pupil. Blue spots near the tail. Female shows more black and more blue with smaller yellow spots.

Below: Hindwing has two rows of orange spots with blue between. Also shows an orange eyespot at trailing edge. Forewing is dark with two rows of yellow spots.

Similar Species: The Spicebush Swallowtail and the female Eastern Tiger Swallowtail (black form) both have black wings but only one row of yellow spots across the top of the hindwings. Neither of these species are found in our area.

Life Cycle: Two broods each year is the norm. Summer pupae about one month. Flight periods from mid May to June and mid July to early September.

Eggs: On parsley and other members of the carrot family.

Caterpillar: Mature larvae are white to leaf-green and sport a black band with rows of yellowish-orange spots. Head is black and white. Young larvae mimic bird droppings.

Chrysalis: Woodlike. Brown or green. May be suspended from building ledges.

Wintering: Overwinters as chrysalis. Summer pupae about one month.

Caterpillar Food: Members of the carrot family: parsley, dill, carrot, celery, parsnip, water parsnip, water hemlocks, sweet cicelies, cow parsnip.

Adult Food: Common milkweed, downy phlox, lilac, clovers and thistles. Males may get moisture and nutrients from damp soil.

Black Swallowtail taking up moisture from wet sand with its tongue (proboscis).

Subfamily: SWALLOWTAILS *Papilioninae* **19**

Canadian Tiger Swallowtail *Papilio canadensis*

MAY	JUNE	JULY	AUGUST	SEPTEMBER

Deciduous to mixed woodlands, pine barrens, forest edges and stream margins.

Nature Notes:

May mate and produce hybrids with the Eastern Tiger Swallowtail in southern Minnesota, southern Wisconsin, lower Michigan and southern New England where the two species overlap.

Description: Wingspan is 3 to 4 inches.

Above: Broad black stripes on pale yellow background. Thick black bands on edges of forewing subtended by nearly continuous yellow band ↑. Red spots near central base on hindwing. "Tails" on hindwings.

Below: Similar to above but with a continuous yellow band along edge of forewing. Long broad black stripe along margin of hindwing. Red spots on edge of hindwing.

Similar Species: Eastern Tiger Swallowtail is larger and more yellow above. It also shows yellow spots on forewing edge instead of a nearly solid yellow band. This is the southern cousin of our Canadian Tiger Swallowtail.

Life cycle: One brood each summer. Flight period from mid May to mid July.

Eggs: Yellowish-green and globular.

Caterpillar: Young caterpillar is brown and white, resembling bird droppings. Mature caterpillar is dark green with two large eyespots on the enlarged thoracic area.

Chrysalis: Mottled green to sticklike brown.

Wintering: Overwinters as chrysalis.

Caterpillar Food: Quaking aspen, birches, willows and maybe ash leaves. Most feeding is done at night.

Adult Food: Cherry blossoms, honeysuckles, lilac, blackberries, American red raspberry, Labrador tea, wild iris, wood lily, spotted joe-pye weed, spreading dogbane, clovers, thistles, milkweeds.

Are those really its eyes? No. The Tiger Swallowtail caterpillar's eyespots merely mimic eyes and may help in scaring off potential predators.

Males frequently congregate in large numbers (up to 100) for moisture and nutrients on damp soil along trails or streams.

Larry's Phenology Records

May 21st is the earliest date I have recorded these swallowtails on the wing. The ten-year average is May 28th.

Once, while on a north country canoe trip, I watched as Tiger Swallowtails fed at the fish-cleaning site and the latrine area.

"The boys at the bar"...sand bar, that is. Males emerge before females and head straight for wet soil. Here they replenish fluids lost during emergence. This clustering, which takes place in the north during late May and early June, facilitates mating as the females can easily locate males.

Cabbage White

Orange Sulphur

Pink-edged Sulphur

Whites and Sulphurs Family Pieridae

About 1200 species worldwide are in this family. Most are found in the tropics, but 65 kinds live in North America. They are medium-sized butterflies with six fully developed legs. Most are white, yellow or orange, but often show seasonal variation. Adults usually bask with closed or folded wings. They take nectar but males will also go to puddles.

Eggs are vase-shaped and are placed singly on food plants. The cylindrical caterpillars are covered with short hairs. Caterpillars of whites prefer plants of the mustard family while the sulphurs go for legumes (pea family). The chrysalis is upright and attached by a cremaster and a silken girdle. Most overwinter as a chrysalis, but some as caterpillars.

Whites (Subfamily Pierinae)

Butterflies are white with black patterns and may exhibit slight sexual dimorphism. Adults will nectar on flowers. They have long antennae. The green caterpillars feed on members of the mustard family. Flight time may be from early spring to late summer; two or three generations. They overwinter as a chrysalis.

24 Mustard White
26 Cabbage White

Sulphurs (Subfamily Coliadinae)

Most are yellow, but females may be white or pale. Adults have short antennae. Some form continuous broods and may show seasonal variations. Young males can be found at moist sites, but also nectar frequently. The green, laterally-striped caterpillars feed on legumes. Winter is spent as a caterpillar.

28 Clouded Sulphur
30 Orange Sulphur
32 Pink-edged Sulphur

Mustard White *Pieris napi*

MAY	JUNE	JULY	AUGUST	SEPTEMBER

Northern deciduous or coniferous (mixed) forests, shrubby wetlands, moist woods, forest openings, trails, roadsides and open fields.

Nature Notes:

May be found all the way north to the arctic.

Spring broods more likely in woods. Summer broods more likely in the open. Summer brood more common.

Species is highly variable and may actually be more than one species.

Prefer to nectar at yellow and white flowers.

Description: Wingspan is 1⅜ to 1¾ inches.

Mostly white with some mustard color on the undersides.

Above: Spring specimen: White with some veins lined in darker markings ↑. Summer specimen: White with no vein markings.

Below: Spring specimens exhibit a striking pattern with veins outlined with dark green-black; especially on the hindwing. May show some yellow (mustard color). Summer specimens are pure white; veins not outlined.

Similar Species: Cabbage White is also white but has one (male) or two (female) black spots on upper forewing.

Note the absence of vein markings on the topside of the Mustard White's wings.

Life Cycle: Two broods each year is the norm. Flight periods are mid May to mid June and early July to late August.

Eggs: Single, pale green and vase-shaped. Placed on undersides of host plant leaves.

Caterpillar: Green with lateral yellow stripes.

Chrysalis: Green or tan and flecked with black.

Wintering: Overwinters as chrysalis.

Cabbage Whites (shown below) can resemble the summer Mustard White if the forewing spot is hidden.

Caterpillar Food: Plants of the mustard family: rock-cresses, winter-cresses and other mustards.

Adult Food:
Blueberry, cherry and wild plum blossoms. Mustards, spreading dogbane, boneset, thistles. More likely on yellow and white flowers.

Cabbage White *Pieris rapae*

MAY	JUNE	JULY	AUGUST	SEPTEMBER

Open or sparsely wooded terrain, gardens, roadsides, farmlands and suburban yards

Nature Notes:

Introduced from Europe into Quebec about 1860. One of only two alien butterflies that have become widespread in this country. The other is the European Skipper.

Males patrol small areas day after day. Courting is a midday affair.

Description: Wingspan is 1½ to 2 inches.

White with dark spots near center of forewing. Also black at tip (apex) of upper forewing.

Above: Forewing is white with one (males) or two (females) dark spots near center of forewing ↑. Black on apex of forewing. Hindwing is all white.

Below: Forewing shows spots as above but no black tip. Apex is more yellowish-green. Hindwing is all white.

Similar Species: Clouded and Orange Sulphurs have white female forms, but both lack spot patterns on forewing and show black borders in flight. Mustard White is all white with no spots above and underside hindwing veins outlined in gray-green.

Cabbage White on a favorite food; a member of the mustard family.

Life cycle: Three broods each year is possible. Long flight season from mid May to mid September.

Eggs: Pale green, elongated eggs.

Caterpillar: Green with faint yellow lines on back and sides; short fine hairs.

Chrysalis: Greenish-tan with short pointed frontal projection.

Wintering: Overwinters as chrysalis.

Caterpillar Food: Plants of the mustard family: mustards, peppergrass, cabbage, broccoli, brussel sprouts, kale, cauliflower, radishes.

Adult Food: Many plants including catnip, purple loosestrife, spreading dogbane, mustards, red clover, hedge nettles, mints, wild bergamot, self-heal, dandelion, spotted knapweed, asters and goldenrods. Often found at mud puddles sucking up moisture and nutrients.

Subfamily: WHITES *Pierinae*   **27**

Clouded Sulphur *Colias philodice*

| MAY | JUNE | JULY | AUGUST | SEPT | OCT |

Open fields, roadsides, moist meadows, suburban areas, lawns.

Nature Notes:

Newly emerged males may go to wet spots for replenishing moisture.

Adults of last summer or spring's generations are smaller and more greenish-yellow.

Clouded Sulphurs may hybridize with Orange Sulphurs.

Description: Wingspan is 1½ to 2½ inches.

Above: Yellow. All wings bordered by black ↑. Black spots on each forewing ↑. These field marks can only be seen when they are in flight. Orange spots on hindwing. Females have yellow spots within the black borders. Rarely seen in spreadwing posture.

Below: Yellow, not orange, and does show some pink on edges. White spots underneath hindwings are usually double and always ringed with pink ↑. Black spots on the forewing. Females may be in a white "alba" form but will still exhibit full black borders on upper wings.

Similar Species: Orange Sulphur is orange above, not yellow. Pink-edged Sulphur has a black cell spot, smaller on the forewing, and a single silver cell spot on underside hindwing. Also, as their name implies, wings are edged with a well-defined pink border.

An Assassin Bug makes a meal of a Clouded Sulphur. The diagnostic black border and spot are usually only seen in flight since they rarely bask with spread wings.

Life Cycle: Three broods each year is possible. Flight period is from early May to late October.

Eggs: Usually laid on red clover, vetches and other legumes.

Caterpillar: Green with lateral white stripes edged in black. Possibly red spots on the white stripe.

Chrysalis: Green but loses its color over time.

Wintering: Overwinters as chrysalis.

Caterpillar Food: Legumes: white clover, bird's-foot trefoil, alfalfa, sweetclovers, vetches.

Adult Food: Dandelion, alfalfa, red clover, goldenrods, asters, mints, blazing-stars.

Orange Sulphur *Colias eurytheme*

MAY	JUNE	JULY	AUGUST	SEPTEMBER

Open fields, roadsides, lawns, cut-over areas; clovers and alfalfa fields.

Nature Notes:

Abundant in cultivated fields.

Originally a southern species, but has moved north during the last century.

Some females may be white (as in Clouded Sulphurs).

May hybridize with Clouded Sulphurs in late summer.

Sometimes roosts in small groups.

Caterpillars feed at night.

Description: Wingspan is 1½ to 2½ inches.

Yellow-orange with black borders above and yellow-orange below. Rarely seen with wings spread.

Above: Forewing is yellow-orange with thick black borders. A black spot is found near the center of yellow-orange. Female may have light spots in the dark border which may make the border appear broken. Hindwing is yellow-orange with thick black borders. Bright orange central patch.

Below: Forewing and hindwing undersides are also yellow-orange but with no black border. They may also show a line of black spots ↑. Two white eyespots are very close to each other; one larger than the other.

Similar Species: Clouded Sulphur is not as orange above. Pink-edged Sulphur is not as orange above and has well-defined pink edges and a single central spot on hindwing below.

Life Cycle: One to three broods each year. Flight period from late May to early September. Peak in late July, early August. Broods may overlap giving the appearance of a single brood.

Eggs: White and spindle-shaped. Laid singly on leaf of host plant.

Caterpillar: Dark green with lateral white line subtended by black.

Chrysalis: Green with short pointed head projections.

Wintering: Overwinters as chrysalis.

Caterpillar Food: Alfalfa, white clover, white sweetclover, vetches.

Adult Food: Alfalfa, red clover, common milkweed, spreading dogbane, blue vervain, spotted joe-pye weed, dandelion, asters, blazing-stars, goldenrods, sunflowers. May also congregate in large numbers at mud puddles for nutrients and moisture.

Pink-edged Sulphur *Colias interior*

MAY	JUNE	JULY	AUGUST	SEPTEMBER

Heath barrens, bogs, meadows, oak-pine barrens, trails, road-sides, beaver meadows, dry fields; burnt and logged areas.

Nature Notes:

Restricted to the northern parts of U.S. where blueberry plants are found.

Young males gather at mud puddles but also take nectar. Females stay closer to trees and food plants.

Description: Wingspan is 1½ to 2 inches.

A gorgeous sulphur that can be found anywhere wild blueberries grow. Yellow with dark borders and pink fringes ↑. Rarely lands with wings spread.

Above: Males are yellow with dark borders and well-defined pink fringes. Post median spots. Females are also yellow but with paler borders. Both have an orange spot on hindwing.

Below: Forewing undersides are light yellow with a single post median pink spot outlined in black. Hindwing shows a single pink-rimmed silver spot ↑. Hindwing undersides may be a greenish-yellow.

Similar Species: Clouded Sulphur has a double hindwing central spot and not as much pink on wing edges.

Life Cycle: Since this butterfly is so intimately tied to its host plant–blueberries–only one

brood is possible each year. Flight period from early June to late August.

Eggs: Pitcher-shaped. Laid on blueberry plants.

Caterpillar: Yellow-green with light dorsal stripes and red-black lateral lines.

Chrysalis: Green. Held to its substrate by a silk girdle.

Wintering: Overwinters as a caterpillar then resumes feeding in spring. Chrysalis formed in late spring.

Caterpillar Food: Blueberries...and only blueberries. Leaves of late sweet blueberry.

Adult Food: Common milkweed, fireweed, spotted knapweed, orange hawkweed, sarsaparillas, asters, goldenrods.

Blueberry plants define the range of this butterfly. Pink-edged Sulphurs depend on them in several stages of life. The adults lay eggs on the leaves and once they hatch, the caterpillars feed on the leaves.

American Copper

Bog Copper

Banded Hairstreak

Eastern Tailed-Blue

Spring Azure

Coppers, Hairstreaks & Blues (Gossamer-wings) Family Lycaenidae

This family has about 6000 species worldwide with a hundred or so making their home in North America. Males of these small butterflies have reduced forelegs; using only four for walking. Females have six normal legs.

Flattened turban-shaped eggs are deposited singly. The caterpillars are flattened and sluglike. They give off honeydew and so therefore are protected by the ants that harvest it. The rounded compact chrysalis is found in the leaf litter. Winter is spent as an egg, caterpillar or chrysalis.

Coppers (Subfamily Lycaeninae)

This is mostly a northern subfamily. Butterflies are brown with a purple sheen. Females may be orange. Adults will nectar at flowers in bogs, swamps and meadows. Caterpillars feed on members of the rose and buckwheat families. They overwinter as eggs.

36 American Copper   42 Dorcas Copper
38 Bronze Copper   44 Purplish Copper
40 Bog Copper

Hairstreaks and Elfins (Subfamily Theclinae)

These small butterflies are dark or iridescent blue above, lighter below. They often have one or two hairlike tails on the hindwings. Many perch upside down and rub the hindwings. They frequently nectar. Caterpillars feed on leaves, flowers and fruits of many plants and may be attended by ants since they give off honeydew. Overwinter as eggs or chrysalis.

46 Coral Hairstreak
48 Edwards' Hairstreak
50 Banded Hairstreak

Blues (Subfamily Polyommatinae)

Males of these small butterflies are blue while the females are brown or gray. They take nectar, but may also congregate at wet sand or mud. Caterpillars are slug-shaped. They feed on legumes and may be attended by ants. Overwinter as eggs, caterpillars or more likely, the chrysalis.

52 Eastern Tailed-Blue
54 Spring Azure
56 Silvery Blue

American Copper   *Lycaena phlaeas*

MAY	JUNE	JULY	AUGUST	SEPTEMBER

Disturbed areas, fields, power-line cuts.

Nature Notes:

May have been introduced from Europe during colonial times, but there is no way to be sure.

Can be quite aggressive toward large butterflies.

Description: Wingspan is 1 to 1⅛ inches.

Orange and dark gray.

Above: Forewing is orange with black spots ↑ and a purplish-dark border. Hindwing is dark gray with an orange submarginal band.

Below: Forewing is orange with white-encircled black spots ↑ and a white margin. Hindwing is light with small black spots and a narrow wavy marginal band.

Similar Species: Bronze Copper is larger, more purple above and less orange. Below it shows more orange on the hindwing. Purplish Copper is also larger with orange on both forewing and hindwing above and more orange below.

Life Cycle: Two or three broods each year is possible. Flight period from mid May to mid September.

American Copper in spreadwing posture on a clover head. This gives one a clue as to their diminutive size.

American Copper on a favorite nectar source; ox-eye daisy.

Eggs: Pale green with ribs.

Caterpillar: Green to rose-red covered with short hairs; some with red dorsal stripes. Caterpillars take three weeks to form a chrysalis.

Chrysalis: Light brown, tinged with pale yellow-green and spotted with black.

Wintering: Overwinters as a chrysalis under leaves or rocks.

Caterpillar Food: Sheep sorrel, curly dock.

Adult Food: Clovers, yarrow, orange hawk-weed, ox-eye daisy, goldenrods, buttercups.

Bronze Copper   *Lycaena hyllus*   (female)

MAY	JUNE	JULY	AUGUST	SEPTEMBER

Low wet meadows, marshes, bogs, ditches, river floodplains, pond edges; streams bordered with sedges and wild iris.

Nature Notes:

Male is more iridescent.

Do not stray much from food plants.

Males do not nectar as readily as females.

Description: Wingspan is 1 to 1½ inches. Larger than most coppers. Purple and orange.

Above: Male's wings are light purple. Hindwing outlined with a dark border. All wings have black spots. By contrast, female's forewing is yellow-orange with dark spots bordered by purple ↑. Her hindwing is purple edged in orange.

Below: Forewing is orange with black spots and white border. Hindwing is white with black spots and a wide orange border ↑.

Similar Species: American Copper is smaller, brighter orange above and shows less orange on hindwing below. Gray Copper shows much less orange below (none on forewing) and is gray above.

Life Cycle: Two broods each year is the norm. Flight periods from mid June to late July and mid August to early September.

Though not a frequent nectarer, Bronze Coppers may be found on flower heads such as this clover. Note wide orange band on hindwing below. This is a diagnostic trait.

Eggs: Pale green and turban-shaped. Found singly on water dock and knotweeds.

Caterpillar: Bright yellowish-green with dark lines down the back.

Chrysalis: Pale orange-brown with dark patches.

Wintering: Overwinters as eggs.

Caterpillar Food: Water dock, curly dock, knotweeds.

Adult Food: Usually not at flowers, but may rarely nectar from alfalfa, red clover, blackberries and milkweeds.

Bog Copper *Lycaena epixanthe* (male)

MAY	JUNE	JULY	AUGUST	SEPTEMBER

Acid bogs with wild cranberries.

Nature Notes:

Low, weak flier.

Adulthood coincides with the flowering of cranberries in the bogs.

Found in relatively small numbers.

Description: Wingspan is ⅞ to 1 inch.

Tiny copper with smaller and fewer spots above ↑.

Above: Dull brown-gray with black spots. Central dark spots on forewing. Male shows fewer spots and is more purplish iridescent than female which is more gray-brown.

Below: Pale yellow-orange to nearly white. Black dots and dashes with orange crescents along edge of hindwing.

Similar Species: Dorcas Copper is darker above and more copper-orange below. It is also a bit larger than the Bog Copper.

Life Cycle: Like other species that are so closely connected to their host plant, in this case cranberries, only one brood is produced each summer. Flight period from early July to mid August.

Though almost exclusively found in bogs with cranberries, they can also be seen in upland areas. This Bog Copper is visiting a blooming yarrow.

Eggs: Deposited on cranberry leaves.

Caterpillar: Blue-green with a dark-green dorsal band, slanted dashes and a light lateral line.

Chrysalis: Green and speckled with black spots. Can be solid purple. Formed on cranberry leaves near the ground.

Wintering: Overwinters as eggs.

Caterpillar Food: Large-fruited cranberries.

Adult Food: Mostly cranberry, but also some bog goldenrod, pearly everlasting, spotted knapweed, yarrow, ox-eye daisy.

Dorcas Copper *Lycaena dorcas* (male)

MAY	JUNE	JULY	AUGUST	SEPTEMBER

Spruce-tamarack bogs, marshes, wet meadows, lake margins, open areas near small streams, brushy old fields.

Nature Notes:

A very northern copper whose range is restricted by the range of its favorite host plant; shrubby cinquefoil.

Females emerge a few days after males.

They seldom stray far from their host plants.

Weak flight.

Description: Wingspan is ¾ to 1⅛ inches.

A tiny, brightly-colored sprite of the spruce-tamarack bogs.

Above: Male's forewing is iridescent purple ↑, dotted with black spots and has a black border. Hindwing is similar with an orange spot on rear margin. Female forewing is rusty brown with black spots. Hindwing is similar, with orange check marks on margin ↑.

Below: Forewing is yellowish-orange with long black dash. Hindwing is light orange-brown, has small black spots and a zigzag orange sub-margin.

Similar Species: Purplish Copper is very similar below, but more orange above and larger. Bog Copper shows a similar pattern below but is lighter gray-brown above. It is also tinier than

Dorcas Coppers show strong sexual dimorphism; males are iridescent purple while females (pictured left) are a much more subtle tone.

Below. Their tiny size is evident when you see one sitting on a Labrador tea leaf.

the Dorcas Copper.

Life Cycle: One brood each summer. Flight period from late June to late August.

Eggs: Flattened greenish-white. Placed singly on shrubby cinquefoil plants.

Caterpillar: Light green with a dark green, mid dorsal line and slight traces of a white line.

Chrysalis: Green, black, brown and even purple with pale stripes along sides. Created in the spring.

Wintering: Overwinters as eggs which have fallen to the ground.

Caterpillar Food: Shrubby cinquefoil, marsh cinquefoil.

Adult Food: Mainly shrubby cinquefoil. Also black-eyed susan.

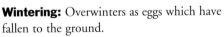

Purplish Copper *Lycaena helloides* (male)

| MAY | JUNE | JULY | AUGUST | SEPTEMBER |

Roadsides, fields, disturbed areas, sedge marshes, wet fields, near streams.

Nature Notes:

Mainly a western and northwest species.

Females are larger than males.

Description: Wingspan is 1 to 1¼ inches.

Males are purplish above and orange below. Females, on the other hand, are orange and black above and orange below.

Above: Male forewings are iridescent purple with black spots and a black border. Hindwing is purple with black spots and an orange zigzag along entire trailing margin ↑. Female forewings are bright orange with black spots and a solid black border. Hindwings are also orange with black spots, but with an orange zigzag along entire trailing margin ↑. All wings are dark near the body.

Below: Male and female forewing undersides are yellow-orange with many tiny black spots. Hindwing is more brown with an orange-on-orange zigzag margin ↑.

Similar Species: Bog Copper is lighter above and below and smaller overall. The Dorcas

**The female Purplish Copper is anything but purple.
Don't be confused by male and female differences.**

Copper is similar below but shows much less orange above (both male and female).

Life Cycle: Two broods each year is the norm. Flight periods from late May to mid June and mid July to late August.

Eggs: Slightly flattened and white. Laid on species of dock and knotweeds.

Caterpillar: Green with a number of lateral slanted yellow lines; covered with short hairs.

Chrysalis: Greenish-gray marked with gray and brown. Stubby.

Wintering: Overwinters as eggs.

Caterpillar Food: Docks, knotweeds.

Adult Food: Clovers, New Jersey tea, peppergrass, milkweeds, asters, goldenrods.

Copper identification in the field is a demanding exercise. Try and see their topsides for easier identification.

Coral Hairstreak *Satyrium titus (male left and female)*

MAY	JUNE	JULY	AUGUST	SEPTEMBER

Brushy fields, orchards, forest edges, meadows, roadsides.

Nature Notes:

Caterpillars hide during the day in leaf litter at the base of host plant. Here they are tended by ants who gather the honeydew they excrete.

The male's wings are more triangular than the females.

Description: Wingspan is 1 to 1¼ inches.

Brown with prominent marginal row of red-orange spots on under hindwing. Lacks tails that are common in other hairstreaks.

Above: Dull brown. Male has oval scent patch near leading edge of forewing. Most females have a row of orange spots near the outer row of the hindwing. Rarely seen with wings spread.

Below: Forewing and hindwing undersides dotted with small white-edged black spots ↑. Prominent band of eight red-orange spots on under hindwing ↑.

Similar Species: Banded Hairstreak shows less orange, more blue and many white crescents beneath. Edward's Hairstreak has less orange, more blue and bigger spots. Acadian Hairstreak is lighter below with paler orange spots. All the above also have tails which the Coral Hairstreak lacks.

Life Cycle: One brood each summer. Flight period from late June to late August.

Eggs: Grayish-white to green.

Caterpillar: Light green with reddish patches near head. Covered in downy hair.

Chrysalis: Light brown with black or dark brown speckles; short brown hairs.

Wintering: Overwinters as eggs.

Caterpillar Food: Will feed on flowers and fruits of chokecherry, wild plum, juneberries.

Adult Food: Spreading dogbane, common milkweed, swamp milkweed, clovers, white sweetclover, meadowsweet, wild strawberries, blackberries, black-eyed susan, spotted knapweed.

Edwards' Hairstreak *Satyrium edwardsii*

MAY	JUNE	JULY	AUGUST	SEPTEMBER

Oak woodland openings and oak thickets in sandy barrens.

Nature Notes:

More southern and usually earlier than other hairstreaks.

Always near oaks which it relies on for egg laying. The caterpillars feed on young red oak or bur oak leaves.

Caterpillars tended by ants at the base of host plants.

Description: Wingspan is 1 to 1¼ inches. Light gray-brown above and below.

Above: Brown without distinguishing features. Hairlike tufts on hindwing.

Below: Brown with rows of elongated spots surrounded by white ↑. Prominent orange crescent at outer angle of under hindwing. Light blue patch near tail is not capped with orange ↑. Postmedian row of separate oval dark brown spots.

Similar Species: Banded Hairstreak shows less orange and no white-lined spots. Acadian Hairstreak has more orange and is lighter with black dots not elongated. Additionally, blue tailspot is capped with orange. Striped Hairstreak is darker and has wide white-lined bars on underwings.

Edwards' Hairstreaks, like all hairstreaks, are
rarely seen in the spreadwing posture.

Life Cycle: One brood each summer. Flight
period from late June to mid August.

Eggs: Found in crevices near buds of oak
saplings. Hatch in May.

Caterpillar: Dark brown with pale yellow
markings. Black head with narrow white stripes.
Feeds on buds before leaves come out. Tended
by ants at the base of host plants during the
day. Young feed in the daytime. Mature caterpillars feed at night.

Chrysalis: Dull yellow-brown mottled with
many darker spots.

Wintering: Overwinters as eggs.

Caterpillar Food: Leaves of young red or bur
oaks.

Adult Food: Spreading dogbane, milkweeds,
vetches, white sweetclover, New Jersey tea,
meadowsweet, staghorn sumac, goldenrods,
spotted joe-pye weed.

Banded Hairstreak *Satyrium calanus*

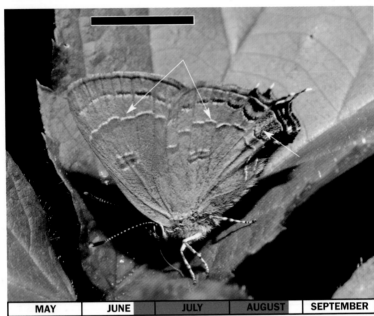

MAY	JUNE	JULY	AUGUST	SEPTEMBER

Open fields next to oak woods, open woods, old fields, parks, roadsides.

Nature Notes:

Common in eastern United States where most oaks are, but can be difficult to tell from other hairstreaks.

Description: Wingspan is 1 to 1¼ inches.

Brown above and dark gray below.

Above: Brown to light brown with oval medial spots on male's forewing.

Below: Dark gray-brown. Post medial dark spots are more elongated with white lines on only one side ↑ that nearly connect to form a line. Blue patch is not capped with orange ↑. Only one or two orange spots near the tail.

Similar Species: Edwards' Hairstreak shows underwing spots encircled with white. Striped Hairstreaks have wider underwing bands. Acadian Hairstreak is lighter with more black dots. All three species show more orange than the Banded Hairstreak.

Life Cycle: One brood each summer. Flight period from late June to late August.

Eggs: Pale green. Laid exclusively on oaks.

Caterpillar: Green with white slanted lines. Feed on oak catkins. Turn brown before forming a chrysalis.

Chrysalis: Hairy, mottled brown.

Wintering: Overwinters as eggs. Hatch as the oak buds open in spring.

Caterpillar Food: Exclusively oaks in our area. South of us they will occasionally utilize butternut, hickory and walnut.

Adult Food: Staghorn sumac, meadowsweet, spreading dogbane, common milkweed, swamp milkweed, yarrow, sweetclovers, dogwoods, fleabanes.

Eastern Tailed-Blue   *Everes comyntas*

| MAY | JUNE | JULY | AUGUST | SEPTEMBER |

Open areas, old fields, pastures, forest clearings, power cuts, roadsides.

Nature Notes:

Low flight.

Rarely rests with spread wings.

Larvae are usually not attended by ants. This is in contrast to its cousins, the Spring Azure and Silvery Blue, whose caterpillars are attended by ants.

Description: Wingspan is ¾ to 1 inch.

Iridescent blue-black above. White below. Very thin tails ↑.

Above: Male is blue with black borders on all wings. Orange spots near tail on hindwing. Female: All wings are dark gray-brown (slightly bluer in spring). Like male, hindwing has orange spots near tail.

Below: Light gray-white with black spots. Hindwing shows two orange spots near tail ↑.

Similar Species: Spring Azure sports neither tail nor orange spots on hindwing. Western Tailed-Blue (which does overlap in Minnesota) is larger, shows very faint orange near tail and has fewer black spots below.

Life Cycle: Three broods each year are possible. Flight period from mid May to early September.

A rare spreadwing pose for the Eastern Tailed-Blue. The darker blue wings indicates a female. Below. A newly emerged adult replenishes fluids at the streambank.

Eggs: Pale green and deposited in flower buds and stems.

Caterpillar: Dark green with brown dorsal stripes, slanted lateral stripes and short hairs.

Chrysalis: Whitish-green with dark head and thorax.

Wintering: Overwinters as a caterpillar in seed pods of food plant.

Caterpillar Food: Legumes (pea family): vetches, clovers, alfalfa, yellow sweetclover, wild peas, milk-vetches, beggar's-ticks. Feed on flowers and buds.

Adult Food: White sweetclover, white clover, beggar's-ticks, spreading dogbane, cinquefoil, wild strawberries, winter-cresses, asters, fleabanes, goldenrods. Newly emerged males may take moisture from wet soil along streams or roads.

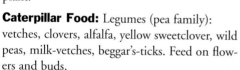

Subfamily: BLUES *Polyommatinae* | 53

Spring Azure   *Celastrina ladon* (male)

APRIL	MAY	JUNE	JULY	AUGUST

Woodland trail edges, pine barrens, forest edges, bogs, swamps, overgrown fields.

Nature Notes:

First spring butterfly in our region to emerge from a chrysalis.

Though usually thought to be one species, may actually be several.

Caterpillars feed on leaves of dogwood, cherries and viburnum. Here these larvae are discovered by ants, and in one of nature's symbiotic relationships, are cared for by the ants until they form a chrysalis.

Description: Wingspan is 1 to 1¼ inches.

Above: Males solid blue. Female is also blue but with black borders on forewing. Checkered margin on both male and female ↑.

Below: White to pale gray with various dark spots ↑.

Similar Species: Eastern Tailed-Blue has orange spots above and below and tails.

Life Cycle: Only one brood each summer. Flights from late April to mid July. Females may live only four days. They mate on day one, lay eggs on day two. Summer broods may hatch later.

Eggs: Deposited among flower buds of chokecherry, blueberries and Labrador tea.

The Spring Azure is the North Woods' gorgeous little harbinger of spring.

"The Spring Azure is not the first butterfly to appear in the spring. This honor belongs to other butterflies that hibernate as adults. However, it is the first butterfly to emerge from its chrysalis.

Mating and laying eggs are about all that can happen in the short life of this little blue butterfly. The adult stage lasts only a week or two, and then the Spring Azure will exit before most butterflies enter for the season."

Backyard Almanac

Caterpillar: Light green to pinkish with green lateral stripes. Attended by ants for honeydew.

Chrysalis: Plump, golden-brown.

Wintering: Overwinters as chrysalis. The Spring Azure is the first butterfly to emerge from its chrysalis in spring in our region.

Caterpillar Food: Dogwoods, cherries, viburnums, blueberry leaves, staghorn sumac, redberried elder and possibly black snakeroot and meadowsweet.

Adult Food: Seldom takes nectar; maybe wild plum. May take moisture and minerals from puddles or damp places.

Larry's Phenology Records

April 24th is the earliest date, over the last ten years, that I have encountered the Spring Azure. Their first appearance is usually around May 9th.

Silvery Blue *Glaucopsyche lygdamus* (male)

MAY	JUNE	JULY	AUGUST	SEPTEMBER

Open fields, brushy fields, woodland openings, moist woods, bogs, stream edges, rocky and sandy soil, burned over areas, flowering meadows.

Nature Notes:

More common in the west.

Males emerge about one week before the females.

Caterpillars are attended by various species of ants.

Description: Wingspan is ⅝ to 1¼ inch.

Blue above; dark gray below.

Above: Male is silvery-blue with black borders ↑ (see photo above); Female is duller blue with wider, less distinct borders.

Below: Gray with distinct single row of white-rimmed black spots ↑.

Similar Species: Eastern Tailed-Blue has tails and orange spots on hindwing. Spring Azure is lighter below. Greenish Blue underwings show a smattering of spots which are not defined in rows as in Silvery Blue.

The row of white-rimmed black spots on the undersides of a Silvery Blue is a diagnostic field mark.

Life Cycle: One brood each summer. Flight period from late May to early July.

Eggs: Laid on various legumes: alfalfa, lupines, sweetclovers, bird's-foot trefoil, vetches, vetchling.

Caterpillar: Slug-shaped. Green to purplish with dark dorsal stripe and slanted white dashes. Color may vary with diet.

Chrysalis: Pale brown with small black dots.

Wintering: Overwinters as chrysalis near the host plant.

Caterpillar Food: Feeds on flowers and pods of legumes including alfalfa, vetches, wild peas, sweetclovers and milk-vetches.

Adult Food: Dandelion and blossoms of wild strawberry, blackberry and chokecherry. Maybe other composites and legumes. They also visit damp soil and sand.

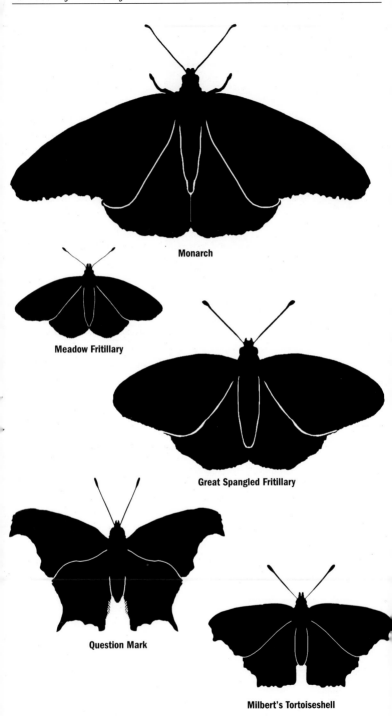

Monarch

Meadow Fritillary

Great Spangled Fritillary

Question Mark

Milbert's Tortoiseshell

Brushfoots
Family Nymphalidae

About 5000 species in the world with 220 in North America. The name "brushfoots" comes from the shortened forelegs that are covered with long hairs. Highly variable group, but most are medium-sized with orange and brown wings that have various shapes. Strong rigid antennae have knobs or clubs on the end. The short proboscis may be used for nectar, but they also feed on sap, dung and rotting fruit.

Eggs are barrel-shaped and placed under the leaves of host plants. Caterpillars have several rows of tubercles and spiny hairs with horn-like structures. Many feed at night when young. The chrysalis hangs by the cremaster. Most brushfoots spend the winter as a caterpillar or chrysalis, but tortoiseshells and anglewings overwinter as adults. Monarchs migrate.

Fritillaries (Subfamily Heliconiinae)

Fritillaries are orange with black patterns. The greater or large fritillaries have forewing undersides similar to their topsides, but have varying metallic spots under the hindwings. The lesser or small fritillaries have more complex undersides with no silver spots. Both are common nectarers in fields and meadows. Caterpillars have banded spines and feed at night on violets. The chrysalis is irregular with dorsal bumps. Fritillaries overwinter as a caterpillar.

Checkerspots, Crescents and Anglewings (Subfamily Nymphalinae)

Checkerspots and crescents are small butterflies that have orange wings with dark markings. The best diagnostic features are on their striking undersides. They nectar on meadow flowers. The caterpillars have rows of spines and tubercles and feed in colonies on composites. Overwinter as a caterpillar. Anglewings include the commas, tortoiseshells, ladies, Question Mark and Mourning Cloak. They are medium-sized and often have wings with many angles. Most are orange and black above; camouflage below. Adults feed on sap, not nectar. Most hibernate as adults. Caterpillars have rows of branching spines and feed on nettles and composites. They form an irregular chrysalis.

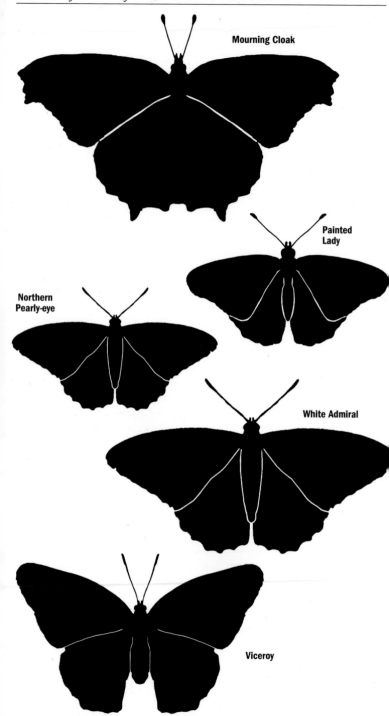

Mourning Cloak

Painted Lady

Northern Pearly-eye

White Admiral

Viceroy

Admirals and Viceroy (Subfamily Limenitidinae)

These medium to large butterflies have distinct bands or spots. They feed on rotting fruits or dung, and regularly go to wet soil. Eggs are placed on cottonwood, aspen and willow leaves. The caterpillars feed on these trees. They overwinter as a caterpillar.

Satyrs and Wood-Nymphs (Subfamily: Satyrinae)

Most satyrs and wood-nymphs are found in woods near water. Medium-sized, most are brown with one or more marginal eyespots. They feed on rotting fruit, dung, sap or go to puddles. Eggs are placed on a host plant. The green-striped caterpillars have forked tails and feed on grasses, rushes and sedges. The chrysalis is round and smooth with two head-horns. It hangs from grass stems. Winter is spent as a caterpillar.

Monarchs (Subfamily Danainae)

Our only member of the Danainae is the Monarch. Large with brightly colored black and orange wings. Forelegs are reduced or stunted in males; forming knobs in females. Adults nectar on many field and meadow flowers. They overwinter as adults that migrate to California and central Mexico. Males have a black scent patch on the middle of the hindwing. Eggs are laid on host plant; milkweeds or dogbanes. Caterpillars feed on these same plants and in turn become distasteful. The chrysalis is rounded with bright dots of gold.

Great Spangled Fritillary *Speyeria cybele*

MAY	JUNE	JULY	AUGUST	SEPTEMBER

Open areas; fields, roadsides, meadows (often moist), forest edges.

Nature Notes:

Most late-season sightings are of females.

Caterpillars feed at night.

Description: Wingspan is 2½ to 3½ inches.

Largest of the fritillaries. From a distance, their wings appear to be a checkerboard of orange and black.

Above: Two-tone orange-brown with black spots, lines and chevrons. Five dark dashes near forewing base.

Below: Hindwing with many metallic silver spots, most forming two rows separated by a wide yellowish band ↑. Outer silver spots are triangular-shaped.

Similar Species: Aphrodite Fritillary is nearly the same size but black at outer edge of forewing with a narrow band separating silver spots under hindwing. Atlantis Fritillary is smaller and also shows black at outer edge of forewing. It is also restricted to mixed-growth woodlands and bogs

Life Cycle: One brood that hatches in the fall. Flight period from mid June to early September.

Great Spangled Fritillaries have a striking underwing pattern. Note the wide yellowish band that helps distinguish this species.

Eggs: Eggs are deposited at the base of violets.

Caterpillar: Brown-black with a dorsal black line. Also black spines with a red base.

Chrysalis: Mottled with dark brown. Males emerge by mid June. Females come out two to four weeks later. Mate in July. Females may linger into September.

Wintering: Caterpillar overwinters.

Caterpillar Food: Various kinds of violets.

Adult Food: Milkweeds, spreading dogbane, red clover, vetches, wild bergamot, ox-eye daisy, spotted knapweed, black-eyed susan, thistles, spotted joe-pye weed.

Blooming common milkweed attracts many late summer butterflies including the Great Spangled Fritillary.

Aphrodite Fritillary *Speyeria aphrodite*

MAY	JUNE	JULY	AUGUST	SEPTEMBER

Wooded cool areas, bogs, oak-pine barrens, forest edges and openings, upland and dry fields, roadsides.

Nature Notes:

Mostly found in the northeast.

Wide tolerance for different habitats.

Description: Wingspan is 2 to 3 inches.

Medium-sized fritillary. Orange-black above; white spots below.

Above: Forewing is orange with black lines, spots and chevron. Often with black border. Extra black spot at base ↑. Hindwing is orange with fewer black markings; cinnamon-brown in center.

Below: Forewing much like above except for a few light apex spots. Hindwing is dark with many white spots and a narrow cream-colored band ↑ in submargin.

Similar Species: Atlantis Fritillaries are smaller with black spots along a very light band on hindwing below. Great Spangled Fritillaries are larger with less black on the edge of wings and a wider tan-colored band in the submargin of the under hindwing.

**Aphrodite Fritillaries show a narrow pale band between the white spots.
Great Spangled Fritillaries have a wide band.**

Life Cycle: One brood each summer. Flight period from late June to early September.

Eggs: Laid on violets.

Caterpillar: Brownish-black with dorsal black lines and brown spine.

Chrysalis: Blackish-brown with yellow wing cases and a gray abdomen.

Wintering: Overwinters as a caterpillar.

Caterpillar Food: Violets, violets and more violets.

Adults Food: Common milkweed, orange hawkweed, spotted knapweed, blazing-stars, thistles.

"Although adult fritillaries feed in the meadow in late summer, shortly before they die, they go to the woods to deposit eggs on violets. The eggs hatch in the fall, and dormant caterpillars survive the winter. They begin feeding in spring with the growth of new violets, and adults emerge in summer and return to the meadow."

Backyard Almanac.

Atlantis Fritillary   *Speyeria atlantis*

MAY	JUNE	JULY	AUGUST	SEPTEMBER

Open, mixed-growth woodlands, moist meadows, bogs, streamsides, trails, flowery openings among deciduous and coniferous forests.

Nature Notes:

Most northern of all the fritillaries.

Males more active than females.

Description: Wingspan is 2 to 2¾ inches.

Medium-sized fritillary. Black and orange. Darker than other fritillaries.

Above: Orange with numerous black lines, spots and chevrons. Solid black wing margins ↑. Males have darkened veins.

Below: Forewing orange on basal 2/3 with black markings as above. Orange spots near tip ↑. Hindwing has many silver spots on dark brown background. Narrow yellow submarginal band ↑. Triangular light spots along margins.

Similar Species: Aphrodite Fritillary above has less black on wing borders; strong black spot at base of forewing. Below it is darker, more reddish-orange. Silver-bordered Fritillary is smaller with no brown on inner portions of forewing above. Below it shows larger white markings. Great Spangled Fritillary is larger with no black border.

Note distinguishing orange spots near tip of forewing. Submarginal band is much narrower than in Great Spangled Fritillary.

Look for the solid black border on the wing margins to separate this species from other fritillaries.

Life Cycle: One brood each summer. Flight period from late June to late August. (Peak in July.)

Eggs: Honey-yellow. Placed near violets.

Caterpillar: Tan after hatching. Becoming yellow-green with a black dorsal line, green-gray below. Covered with gray spines.

Chrysalis: Brown with black speckles and light brown mottling. Pupation about two weeks long.

Wintering: Overwinters as caterpillar.

Caterpillar Food: Violets.

Adult Food: New Jersey tea, meadowsweet, alfalfa, crown vetch, common milkweed, mints, virgin's bower, fireweed, pearly everlasting, fleabanes, orange hawkweed, yellow hawkweed, spotted knapweed, thistles, burdock, ox-eye daisy, boneset.

Subfamily: FRITILLARIES *Heliconiinae*   **67**

Bog Fritillary *Boloria eunomia*

MAY	JUNE	JULY	AUGUST	SEPTEMBER

Black spruce/tamarack bogs, sphagnum/heath bogs.

Nature Notes:

A northern fritillary found over much of Canada.

Females emerge several days later than the males.

Description: Wingspan is 1¼ to 1½ inches.

One of the smallest fritillaries in the North Woods. More black and less orange than other species in our area.

Above: Orange with black chevrons, lines and spots as seen in other fritillaries, but more black. Note the submarginal row of black spots on forewing and hindwing that appear to be surrounded by orange and boxed in by black ↑.

Below: Forewing is light orange with small spots. Hindwing has a postmedial band of small white spots outlined in black ↑; larger white shapes on anterior and submargin.

Similar Species: Silver-bordered Fritillary shows a postmedian row of black spots on hindwing below and less black above.

Look for the row of round white spots that are unique to the Bog Fritillary.

Life Cycle: One brood each summer. Flight period from mid June to early July.

Eggs: Cream-colored. On wild cranberry, violets, willows.

Caterpillar: Red-brown with branched reddish spines. Head is brownish-yellow.

Chrysalis: Tan or brown.

Wintering: Overwinters as a caterpillar.

Caterpillar Food: Willows, violets, cranberries.

Adult Food: Bog laurel, Labrador tea, dandelion, goldenrods.

Silver-bordered Fritillary *Boloria selene*

MAY	JUNE	JULY	AUGUST	SEPTEMBER

Bogs, wet meadows, marshes, swamps with willows, woodlands near wetlands.

Nature Notes:

Females emerge a week or more later than males.

Found further north in Canada than most fritillaries.

Description: Wingspan is 1½ to 2 inches.

Only small fritillary with metallic silver spots on hindwing below. Orange-black above.

Above: Orange with black lines, spots and chevrons. Not so dark in center. Light border at very edge of wings ↑. Submarginal row of black ↑ and orange spots.

Below: Forewing is orange with black spots and a marginal row of silver spots. Hindwing has several lines of silver polygons including large submarginal silver spots ↑.

Similar Species: Meadow Fritillary's hindwing below lacks large white spots. Bog Fritillary's undersides show white submarginal spots where Silver-bordered has black spots. Most other common fritillaries are larger.

A Silver-bordered Fritillary perches atop a food plant; spreading dogbane.

Life Cycle: Two broods each year is usual. Flight periods from late May to mid June and early July to early August.

Eggs: Cream-colored and placed on or near violets.

Caterpillar: Dark gray with dark blotches and pale yellow spines. Two long thoracic spines.

Chrysalis: Tan with brown and green patches. Dorsal spines on abdomen.

Wintering: Overwinters as caterpillar.

Caterpillar Food: Violets.

Adult Food: Wild iris, Labrador tea, red clover, black-eyed susan, boneset, pearly everlasting, ox-eye daisy, spotted knapweed, dogbanes, thistles, goldenrods, asters.

Meadow Fritillary *Boloria bellona*

MAY	JUNE	JULY	AUGUST	SEPTEMBER

Grassy fields, moist meadows, pastures, streamsides, forest clearings, bogs.

Nature Notes:

Most common member of the lesser fritillaries.

Flies low with rapid jerky zigzag patterns.

Male hovers in front of female.

Description: Wingspan is 1¼ to 2 inches.

Orange with black markings of spots, zigzags and chevrons.

Above: Orange with black markings of spots, zigzags and chevrons. No black borders on wing edges ↑. Forewing with a bit more black than hindwing. Squared off apex of forewing.

Below: Forewing with black markings on orange wings. Apex pale-purple. Hindwing exhibits a pale lavender smudge on the outer half ↑. Brownish-white keel-shaped patch at base of costa.

Similar Species: Silver-bordered Fritillary has a black border above and silver spots below, especially on hindwing. Freija Fritillary's forewing is more pointed and has more black zigzags below hindwing. Frigga Fritillary shows a longer, whitish arrowhead-shaped spot at base of costa.

Lavender wash on the Meadow Fritillaries hindwing undersides is diagnostic.

Life Cycle: Double brooded. Flight periods from mid May to mid June and early July to mid September.

Eggs: Greenish-yellow.

Caterpillar: Shiny green to purple-black with yellow-brown branching spines. V-shaped markings on back.

Chrysalis: Yellow-brown.

Wintering: Overwinters as a caterpillar.

Caterpillar Food: Violets: Woolly blue violet, northern white violet.

Adult Food: Prefers yellow flowers: black-eyed susan, dandelion, goldenrods, ox-eye daisy. Also some red clover, bog rosemary, spreading dogbane, blue vervain.

Silvery Checkerspot *Chlosyne nycteis*

MAY	JUNE	JULY	AUGUST	SEPTEMBER

Floodplains, forest openings, moist meadows, marshes, road-sides, fields, second-growth scrub, sandy areas, old burns, cut-over areas.

Nature Notes:

Often in areas of poor soil.

Flies low and slow.

Caterpillars feed communally.

Description: Wingspan is 1½ to 2 inches.

Black and orange above; lighter below.

Above: More black than orange. Medial orange band bordered by black. Hindwing shows a row of black submarginal spots surrounded by orange; some spots with white centers ↑.

Below: Forewing is pale orange with brown patches and brown margin. Hindwing has white median band; submarginal white band is interrupted with dark patch ↑ and a silvery crescent.

Similar Species: Harris' Checkerspot shows even more black above and is more colorful below. Pearl Crescent is smaller with wider black border and paler below. Gorgone Checkerspot has more orange and white spots above, marginal chevrons; hindwing undersides show large black spots and white chevrons.

To identify a Silvery Checkerspot from its undersides, look for the brown patch that interrupts the white submarginal band.

Life Cycle: One brood each summer. Flight period from mid June to early August.

Eggs: Green-white. Clusters of about 100 on composites (mostly asters and sunflowers).

Caterpillar: Brownish-black with broken yellow lateral stripes and white dots. Covered with black spines. Head is black.

Chrysalis: Yellow-green to gray-brown. Five rows of conical tubercles on abdomen.

Wintering: Overwinters as a caterpillar.

Caterpillar Food: Asters, black-eyed susan, sunflowers.

Adult Food: Common milkweed, staghorn sumac, spreading dogbane, red clover, vetches, fleabanes.

Harris' Checkerspot   *Chlosyne harrisii*

| MAY | JUNE | JULY | AUGUST | SEPTEMBER |

Wet shrubby meadows, moist pastures, wet ditches, bog edges, marshes.

Nature Notes:

Female larger and lighter than male.

Slow flight near food plants.

Colonial caterpillars.

Description: Wingspan is 1¼ to 1¾ inches.

Above: Primarily black on the back with two orange bands and black or dark brown borders. More black than orange above; both on the forewing and hindwing. Row of black dots on hindwing touching wide black margin ↑.

Below: Alternating white and orange-brown bands. Forewing is mostly orange. Hindwing undersides are a checkered pattern of white, orange, reddish-tan and black. Three bands of white spots and crescents. On undersides of both wings look for the complete marginal orange band ↑.

Similar Species: Silvery Checkerspot is similar but hindwing is paler below. No reddish-orange below. Pearl Crescent is smaller, not as black above and not as checkered below on hindwing.

Who said the topsides of butterflies are the prettiest?

Life Cycle: One brood each summer. Flight period from mid June to late July (peak in late June).

Eggs: In clusters of about twenty-five under leaves of flat-topped white asters.

Caterpillar: Colonial. Deep red-orange with dorsal black stripes, cross stripes on each segment; covered with black spines.

Chrysalis: White, spotted with black, brown and orange. Black-tipped tubercles.

Wintering: Overwinters as a caterpillar at base of host plant. Continues feeding in spring.

Caterpillar Food: Flat-topped white aster and occasionally goldenrods.

Adult Food: Spreading dogbane and vetches. Moisture and nutrients from damp soil.

Baltimore Checkerspot *Euphydryas phaeton*

MAY	JUNE	JULY	AUGUST	SEPTEMBER

Marshes and wet meadows with turtlehead, fields with English plantain, open sphagnum bogs, brushy swamps, dry open wooded hills, oak-pine barrens.

Nature Notes:

Named after the black and orange colors worn by Lord Baltimore (as in Baltimore oriole).

Bright coloration may be warning of an unpalatable butterfly. Eating turtlehead plants during the caterpillar stage makes the adults taste bad.

The caterpillars make webs and feed communally.

Description: Wingspan is 1⅝ to 2½ inches.

Dark above, checkered below. Note the colorful body (abdomen) marked with white spots and orange.

Above: Forewing is mostly black with two orange spots on leading edge. Many white spots on submargin with orange border. Hindwing is mostly black with submarginal white spots and that distinctive orange border.

Below: Striking checkerboard pattern of orange, black and white. undersides of both wings similar; checkered white spots in center, basal orange to reddish rectangular spots and orange border. Females are larger than males.

Similar Species: None; but this butterfly may appear all black while in flight.

A mating pair of Baltimore Checkerspots is a stunning sight.

Life Cycle: One brood each summer. Flight period from mid June to mid August.

Eggs: Yellow. Hundreds placed under leaves of turtlehead.

Caterpillar: Orange-red and banded with black. Covered with black spines. Young make webs and feed communally.

Chrysalis: White with black markings and orange dots.

Wintering: Overwinters as a caterpillar in silken nests below host plants on ground.

Caterpillar Food: Before winter they feed on turtlehead, English plantain and beardstongue. In spring they turn to willows and arrowheads.

Adult Food: Shrubby cinquefoil, wild roses, viburnums, spreading dogbane, common milkweed, swamp milkweed, black-eyed susan.

Northern Crescent *Phyciodes selenis* (male)

MAY	JUNE	JULY	AUGUST	SEPTEMBER

Open sites: meadows, grassy areas, streamsides, roadsides.

Nature Notes:

Very similar to Pearl Crescent and may be very hard to distinguish. Formerly they were considered one species. Pearl Crescent is found further south. They do not produce distinct hybrids.

Description: Wingspan is 1 to 1½ inches.

Black and orange with a black border above. Female darker than male. Orange-yellow below. Males have black and orange antenna clubs.

Above: Forewing and hindwing are both black and orange, bordered in black. Hindwing also has a large patch of solid orange ↑. Less black on male. Female is darker.

Below: Light orange-yellow. Forewing has four dark spots. Hindwing is light with dark brown patch at trailing edge ↑. No pearl crescent marking on male, light patch here on female.

Similar Species: Female Pearl Crescent has more black and less open orange on upper hindwing and is smaller. Pearl Crescent's namesake is a white "pearl" or chevron on the trailing edge of the hindwing's underside. Northern Crescents lack this. These two species do not overlap in the Arrowhead of Minnesota, very northern Wisconsin, the U.P. of Michigan or northern New England..

Notice the dark spots on the forewing and the smudgey dark patch at the trailing edge of the hindwing. These field marks help distinguish this species from the similar Pearl Crescent.

Life Cycle: One brood each summer. Flight period from early June to mid August.

Eggs: Pale green. Deposited on the undersides of aster leaves.

Caterpillar: Dark brown with pinkish-gray spines.

Chrysalis: Mottled gray to yellowish-brown.

Wintering: Overwinters as caterpillar.

Caterpillar Food: Asters, especially small blue aster.

Adult Food: Spreading dogbane, white clover, fleabanes, thistles, asters. They will get moisture and nutrients from damp soil.

Question Mark *Polygonia interrogationis*

APRIL	MAY	JUNE	JULY	AUGUST	SEPT	OCT

Woodlands and adjacent open areas, parks, damp meadows, trails, roadsides, streamsides.

Nature Notes:

Widespread in eastern United States.

May estivate in summer.

Populations vary from year to year.

Largest of the anglewings.

Description: Wingspan is 2 to 2¾ inches.

Black-orange above, gray-brown below. Tails on hindwing. Jagged-edged wings.

Above: Forewing is orange with seven black spots in subapical region ↑. Hindwing is orange with few black spots and more reddish-brown. More black in summer form.

Below: Fall form is orange-brown with silver "question mark" on hindwing ↑. Summer form is more brownish.

Similar Species: Commas have one less black spot in subapex of forewing and are usually smaller.

Life Cycle: One to two broods each year in our area. Flight periods from April to late May and early July to October.

Its namesake revealed. The silver "?" on the underside of the hindwing stands out dramatically.

Eggs: Light green and cone-shaped. Deposited on elms, nettle, hackberry and hops.

Caterpillar: Varies from black to yellow with yellowish to red lines. Covered with yellow to reddish hairs and black spines.

Chrysalis: Ranges from yellow to dark brown; deeply notched heads.

Wintering: Overwinters as an adult, in other words, hibernates. May also make a migration.

Caterpillar Food: Nettles, elms, hackberry, hops and maybe basswood.

Adult Food: Tree sap, rotten fruit, dung and carrion. Moisture and nutrients from damp soil and mud. Usually does not nectar, but may visit common milkweed, bog rosemary and asters.

Larry's Phenology Records

April 19th is the earliest I have noted these butterflies. The average date for their first appearance in the Duluth area over the last ten years has been April 30th.

Eastern Comma *Polygonia comma*

MARCH	APRIL	MAY	JUNE	JULY	AUGUST	SEPT	OCT

Moist woodlands, open woods, woodland edges, streamsides, swamps, marshes.

Nature Notes:

Summer form may estivate (go dormant) during hot weather.

Do not migrate but hibernate in hollow trees, etc.

Caterpillars feed at night.

Adults will perch in closed-wing pose, head down; well camouflaged as a dead leaf.

Member of the Anglewings (Subfamily Nymphalinae); which refers to the jagged edge of the wings.

Description: Wingspan is 1¾ to 2 inches.

Orange and black above, brown below.

Above: Forewing has a single dark postmedian spot near the bottom edge on an orange background. Five small spots, one large one on each forewing ↑. Hindwing has dark border enclosing pale spots. Short "tails". On the summer form, the hindwing is darker, nearly all black.

Below: Brown with silver or white comma mark ↑.

Similar Species: Question Mark is larger. It is similar above but with one more black spot on the forewing and has longer "tails". Gray Comma undersides have gray striations. The edges of the Green Comma undersides show submarginal green spots. Satyr Comma is more orange above with one more spot on the forewing. It is also yellow-brown below.

Life Cycle: Two broods each year is the norm.

Note the obvious mark in the shape of a comma on the underside of the hindwing.

Summer flight: late June or July to August.
Winter flight: September to May.

Eggs: Pale green and keg-shaped. Laid on elms, nettle and hops in early spring.

Caterpillar: Variable, black to green-brown and white. Spines are black to white. Yellow tubercles.

Chrysalis: Brown with a few gold or silver lateral spots. Curved so that it may resemble twisted wood.

Wintering: Hibernator; which simply means they overwinter as an adult.

Caterpillar Food: Nettles, wood nettle, hops, elms.

Adult Food: Feeds on tree sap, rotten fruit, decaying organic matter, dung, carrion. Does not usually go to flowers, but may visit common milkweed. Also takes in nutrients and moisture from damp soil.

Larry's Phenology Records

March 26th is the earliest date I have seen the Eastern Comma. Their first appearance averages April 20th in the Duluth area.

Green Comma   *Polygonia faunus*

| MARCH | APRIL | MAY | JUNE | JULY | AUGUST | SEPT | OCT |

Coniferous forests, forest trails and roads, forest openings, rocky glades.

Nature Notes:

Wing margins more jagged than any other comma.

Main range is in Canada.

Adults may go dormant in the summer.

Adults may live nine or ten months.

Description: Wingspan is 1¾ to 2 inches.

Black-orange above and brown below. Very jagged wing margins. The "comma" is a light mark on the underside of the hindwing.

Above: Forewing is orange with seven black costal spots; two on inner margin which may be fused ↑. Black border. Hindwing is orange dotted by three black spots. Five bold yellow spots punctuate the dark border ↑.

Below: Shades of brown with a blue-green submarginal band ↑. Males are more gray than the brownish females. Look for its namesake, the silver comma, on the center of hindwing when at rest.

Similar Species: Gray Comma has a hindwing which is more black above and only shows two black spots. Eastern Comma's forewing marked with one fewer spot above; more orange. Satyr Comma is lighter brown below. Hoary Comma is darker above near the body. All the above lack a green tinge below which is characteristic of the aptly named Green Comma.

The greenish tint to the submargin of the underwings gives this butterfly its name.

Life Cycle:
One brood each summer. Flight periods from late March/early April to early June and late July to October. Adults may live nine or ten months. Adults emerge in mid to late summer, overwinter and reproduce in spring.

Eggs: Pale green and found on speckled alder, birches, blueberries, currants and willows.

Caterpillar: Yellowish-brown to red with white patch near middle. Also shows a broken dull orange band laterally. Head black with white "W" on front.

Chrysalis: Pale brown or tan with dusky green streak and metallic spots.

Wintering: Overwinters as an adult.

Caterpillar Food: Speckled alder, willows, birches, currants, blueberries.

Adult Food: Prefers tree sap, rotten fruit, carrion and dung. Moisture sucked up from damp soil. Usually does not nectar, but some have been seen on dandelions.

Gray Comma *Polygonia progne*

| MARCH | APRIL | MAY | JUNE | JULY | AUGUST | SEPT | OCT |

Rich deciduous woods, open woods, forest edges, swamps, pine barrens, trails, dirt roads, homesteads.

Nature Notes:

Northern butterfly.

Maybe the most widespread of all the Anglewings.

Perches at edge of clearings.

Slow flight.

Description: Wingspan is 1⅝ to 2 inches.

Brown-orange above. Striated gray below.

Above: Forewing is orange with the typical six black spots. Black border with ragged margins. Hindwing has a more reddish center and a wide black border spotted with three to five tiny yellow dots ↑.

Below: Striated gray without whitish outer portions found on other commas. The silver "comma" mark can be √-shaped or fishhook-shaped. On the Gray Comma it is thin and tapers on both ends ↑.

Two seasonal forms; summer form is darker than the fall-spring form.

Similar Species: Eastern Comma is not as dark above and darker below. Green Comma, while similar above, shows a distinctive green

tint on borders below.
Hoary Comma is darker in central area above and darker below. Satyr Comma is much lighter above and lighter, more orangish below. Compton Tortoiseshell exhibits white spots above and no comma below.

Life Cycle: Two broods each year is the norm. Flight periods from mid June to mid August and late September to mid May (hibernating through the winter).

Note how the "comma" mark is thin and tapers at both ends. This is a distinguishing field mark.

Eggs: Green and ribbed. Deposited singly on gooseberry plants.

Caterpillar: Yellow-brown with dark blotches and lines. Head is orange-brown.

Chrysalis: Tan to brown with dark streaks.

Wintering: Hibernator. Overwinters as adult.

Caterpillar Food: American elm, paper birch, gooseberries.

Adult Food: Tree sap, rotting fruit, carrion and dung. Moisture and nutrients from damp soil. Normally does not nectar at flowers but has been observed working on common milkweed.

Compton Tortoiseshell *Nymphalis vaualbum*

MARCH	APRIL	MAY	JUNE	JULY	AUGUST	SEPT	OCT

Various wooded sites; forest openings, edges and trails. Upland boreal forests, especially mature deciduous trees.

Nature Notes:

Subject to cyclical population explosions and possibly migration. Range may be expanding.

Adults live at least nine months.

Butterfly named after Compton County, Quebec.

"Tortoiseshell" refers to the brown-yellow pattern of the wings resembling the mottled appearance of some turtles (such as the hawksbill).

Description: Wingspan is 2¼ to 3 inches.

Mix of black, brown, orange, and yellow with four white spots.

Above: All wings have several black spots and are rusty brown near the body. One white spot on all four wings ↑. Jagged margins with a small tail projection on hindwing.

Below: Mottled light and dark brown.

Similar Species: Gray Comma is smaller and has no white spots. It also shows less black on forewing but more black on hindwing.

Life Cycle: One brood each summer. Adults emerge in late June or early July. Often estivate for the summer. Adults fly in September and October. Mate in early spring (mid March to May). Overwinters as an adult, hibernating in hollow logs or outbuildings.

Jagged wing edges and cryptic coloration underneath allow the Compton Tortoiseshell to blend in with tree bark.

"They commonly hibernate beneath bark or in hollow trees but they readily select cabins and outbuildings as well. One Canadian fishing cabin sheltered thirty of these butterflies tucked behind a window shutter.

Unrolling its long tongue, the Compton Tortoiseshell feeds on dripping sap, about the only food available in early spring [when they first emerge from hibernation].

When frightened or in danger, the butterflies close their wings, letting their camouflaged undersides blend with the tree bark."

Backyard Almanac

Larry's Phenology Records

April 8th is the average date of first appearance. March 22nd is the earliest I have ever seen one. Comptons appear a few days ahead of their cousin, Milbert's Tortoiseshell.

Eggs: Laid on aspens, birches, willows.

Caterpillar: Light green with black spines. They feed communally.

Chrysalis: Brown-green, angled and with a horned head. Hangs from wood.

Wintering: Hibernators. Overwinter in the shelter of hollow trees, under bark or utilize seasonal outbuildings.

Caterpillar Food: Birch, willow and aspen leaves.

Adult Food: Tree sap (especially maple) and rotting fruit. Moisture and nutrients taken up from damp soil. Dung is also utilized.

Milbert's Tortoiseshell *Nymphalis milberti*

MARCH	APRIL	MAY	JUNE	JULY	AUGUST	SEPT	OCT

Woodlands, open fields, meadows, wet pastures, swamp, marsh edges, streams margins, roadside ditches, roads, trails.

Nature Notes:

Named for Milbert; a lepidopterist collecting butterfly specimens in the U.S. during the 1820s.

Found across much of Canada, Milbert's Tortoiseshell is a true northern butterfly.

Populations will vary yearly.

Often near or on the ground.

Description: Wingspan is 1¾ to 2½ inches.

Bright orange and yellow and deep brown with forewing borders. Darker striations below. Outer margins are irregular with short tails.

Above: Bright, two-toned, orange-yellow band bordered with dark brown ↑. Two orange patches on leading edge of each forewing. Black basal areas. Margin spotted with dark blue.

Below: Dark brown with a lighter, wide submarginal band ↑.

Similar Species: Mourning Cloak is nearly double the size. Also its undersides are darker and the light band is on the outer edge, not towards the center.

Life Cycle: Two broods each year is the norm. Flight periods from mid June to mid August and early September to early May (hibernating in winter).

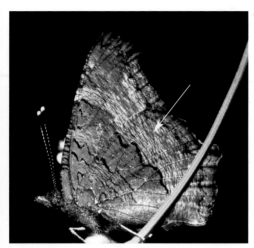

Look for adults as early as March in the north. Adults emerge from hibernation during the first warm sunny days of spring.

"They deposit their eggs on nettles, and the caterpillars feed almost exclusively on the leaves of these plants.

Milbert's Tortoiseshell butterflies stay active in the fall sunlight, visiting hardy flowers and sipping tree sap until late in [September]."

Backyard Almanac

Larry's Phenology Records

April 11th is the average first date on-the-wing over the last ten years in the Duluth area. This is three days later than the average Compton Tortoiseshell date of first appearance. March 27th is the earliest I have recorded them.

Eggs: Pale green. Hundreds clustered on nettles.

Caterpillar: Black with tiny white spots. Broken, greenish-yellow stripes covered with seven rows of black spines. Feeds in groups when young, becoming solitary at maturity. Utilizes folded leaves for shelter.

Chrysalis: Grayish or greenish-tan. Covered with short spines.

Wintering: Overwinters as adult. Hibernate in hollow logs, under bark and old outbuildings.

Caterpillar Food: Nettles.

Adult Food: Alfalfa, vetches, spreading dogbane, willow catkins, lilac, black-eyed susan, boneset, ox-eye daisy, dandelion, spotted knapweed, spotted joe-pye weed, goldenrods, thistles. Also take in sugars and minerals from tree sap, rotten fruit and dung.

Mourning Cloak *Nymphalis antiopa*

Forest openings, edges, swamps, stream margins, meadows, roadsides, parks, gardens, yards.

Nature Notes:

Usually the first butterfly seen in the spring; often when snow still lies on the ground.

Gliding type of flight.

May bask on ground.

Adults are the longevity champions of the butterfly world. They can live ten or eleven months.

Often found at sapsucker feeding holes. These parallel rows of small holes ooze sap and also attract bees, flies and other butterflies.

Description: Wingspan is 3 to 4 inches.

Large dark butterfly with yellow border. Flies very early in the spring.

Above: All dark with cream-yellow borders ↑ and blue submarginal spots.

Below: Dark striated brown with white terminal band ↑.

Similar Species: Milbert's Tortoiseshell is half the size and the submarginal band is orangish. Some moths may also be dark.

Life Cycle: One brood that hatches in spring. Adults estivate and overwinter. Adults hibernate in logs, woodpiles and under loose bark. They wake in early spring. Mate from April to June. Adults emerge in late June and feed and estivate. Wake in late August or September, feed and overwinter. Some migration south.

Usually our earliest butterfly on the wing, the Mourning Cloak can be seen as early as the first week in March. The average emergence date for the Duluth area is April 8th. Oozing sap and rotten fruit keep them going in the early spring.

Larry's Phenology Records

Two years share the record for the earliest Mourning Cloak sighting. On March 7th, 1987 the temperature hit 69 degrees F and I observed a Mourning Cloak on the wing. Thirteen years later, deja vu, on March 7th, 2000, the temperature reached 70 degrees F and I once again saw the first Mourning Cloak of the year. Here are my first sightings over the last ten springs:

1991	April 15
1992	April 30
1993	March 29
1994	April 16
1995	April 22
1996	April 9
1997	April 13
1998	March 28
1999	April 30
2000	March 7

The average works out to April 8th which is tied with Compton Tortoiseshell for the earliest spring dates.

Eggs: Whitish; becoming tan to black before hatching. In groups around tree or bush twigs.

Caterpillar: Black with small white spots, dorsal red dots, black spines.

Chrysalis: Tan-gray.

Wintering: Hibernate as adults. For protection they use hollow logs, woodpiles and loose bark.

Caterpillar Food: Usually willows, but also , hackberry, cottonwood, birches, elms and aspens.

Adult Food: Sap form various trees especially oaks (often found at sapsucker holes). Overripe fruit as well. Minerals and moisture from soils.

American Lady *Vanessa virginiensis*

MAY	JUNE	JULY	AUGUST	SEPT	OCT

Open spaces, fields, meadows, vacant lots, roadsides, forest clearings, streamside.

Nature Notes:

Sometimes called American Painted Lady, Hunter's Butterfly or Virginia Lady.

Adults probably do not survive winter this far north.

Populations vary dramatically from year to year.

Description: Wingspan is 1¾ to 2¼ inches.

Orange-black above and gray and pink below.

Above: Forewing marked by black apex with white spots. Orange with disconnected black median markings. Hindwing is mostly orange with four small black submarginal spots; some with blue centers ↑.

Below: Forewing has a large pink patch. Hindwing undersides look back at you with two distinctively large eyespots ↑ within a masklike pattern. As the saying goes; "American Ladies have big eyes and an open mind." The open mind refers to the "mask" which is unmarked by pale veins. Winter form is smaller and paler.

Similar Species: Painted lady has four smaller eyespots on hindwing below. The eyespots are separated by pale veins.

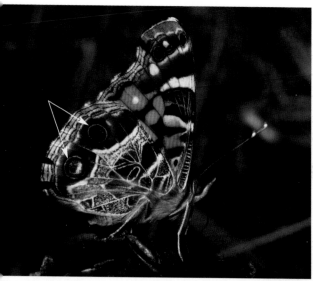

Life Cycle: Two to three broods each year in our area. Flight periods from mid May to mid June and mid July to October.

Eggs: Yellow-green. Deposited singly on pearly everlasting or burdock.

Caterpillar: Alternating black and orange-yellow bands with white dots and covered with blackish spines. Feed solitarily in a leaf nest on host plant. Young larvae feed on leaves while mature larvae feed on flowers.

Chrysalis: Gray-white or bright golden-green marked with purple-brown.

Wintering: Overwinters as chrysalis.

Caterpillar Food: Pearly everlasting, pussy toes, burdock.

Adult Food: Red clover, chokecherry, lilac, bog rosemary, Labrador tea, self-heal, spreading dogbane, common milkweed, orange hawkweed, asters, goldenrods. Newly emerged males may be found at puddles.

American Ladies are said to have "large eyes and an open mind". This is a good field mark and refers to the masklike pattern on the underwings. It separates them from the similar Painted Lady which has four eyespots below within a cobweb-like pattern.

Painted Lady *Vanessa cardui*

MAY	JUNE	JULY	AUGUST	SEPT	OCT

Old fields, meadows, pastures, yards, gardens, parks, roadsides, open forests.

Nature Notes:

Most cosmopolitan butterfly in the world.

"Thistle butterfly" would be an appropriate name for this butterfly since the larvae feed on the leaves of the Canada thistle. The black spiny caterpillars will strip the thistles bare.

Painted Lady populations are variable from year to year. 1993 was an explosion year in Duluth.

Larry's Phenology Records

May 1st is the earliest date I have recorded the Painted Lady in the Duluth area. The ten-year average first date is May 10th.

Description: Wingspan is 2 to 2¼ inches.

Orange and black spots. Pink blotch on underwings.

Above: Orange with black spots and marks. A few white spots on the forewing apex. Black blotch at trailing edge ↑. Hindwing has black lines and spots near borders. Forewing is pointed.

Below: Four small eyespots on the mostly brown hindwing ↑. Forewing undersides blotched with pinkish areas. Brown and white splotches.

Similar Species: American Lady is smaller and shows more orange above with smaller white spots. Also hindwing below has two larger eyespots.

Life Cycle: Two broods each year is the norm. Flight period from May to October.

Eggs: Pale green and barrel-shaped. Placed on thistles, burdock, honeysuckles and possibly asters.

Painted Ladies may be abundant some springs, while nearly absent other years.

Caterpillar: Purple to yellow-green mottled with dark lines on back and yellow stripes on the side. Black head and black spines. Caterpillar makes nest on top of host plant where it feeds.

Chrysalis: Lavender-brown, bumpy and bluntly beaked. Nearly one-inch long. Hangs upside down.

Wintering: Hibernator. Overwinters as an adult. Overwinters in Southwest U.S. or Mexico.

Caterpillar Food: Legumes and composites: burdock, ragworts, spotted knapweed, pearly everlasting, wormwoods.

Adult Food: Blackberries, catnip, Labrador tea, lupines, red clover, milkweeds, spotted joe-pye weed, asters, blazing-stars.

"Painted Ladies are both cyclic and migratory. Being cyclic, they have years of population highs and lows. Being migratory, they winter in the southern United States and return early in the spring. Upon arrival, the adults lay eggs and die by the end of [May]. By late summer, the next generation of Painted Ladies will feed on soil minerals and garden flowers."

Backyard Almanac

Red Admiral *Vanessa atalanta*

MAY	JUNE	JULY	AUGUST	SEPT	OCT

Open areas with flowers, gardens, fields, barnyards, moist meadows, marshes, forest edges, parks, trails.

Nature Notes:

Caterpillars feed on nettles, even the rash-and-itch-causing, stinging nettles.

Rapid flight.

Often territorial and defensive.

Larry's Phenology Records

April 12th is the earliest I have seen this butterfly in the northland. Their average first date of emergence is May 16th.

Description: Wingspan is 1¾ to 2¼ inches.

Dark wings with red bands and white apical spots that resemble an exclamation point. Red bands form a horseshoe-shape when viewed with spread wings.

Above: Forewing is black with a distinctive red submarginal band ↑ and a few white apical marks. Hindwing also black with red band on lower margins (trailing edge) ↑.

Below: Forewing is similar to above forewing but shows pink band ↑. Hindwing is mottled with no red band.

Similar Species: The Painted Lady's forewing below is pink banded and somewhat similar but the hindwing shows very distinct eyes which the Red Admiral lacks. Above is black and orange and very different.

Red Admiral feeding on a favorite nectar source–red clover.

"It may come as a surprise to know that Monarchs are not the only of our butterflies to migrate. Less spectacularly, Red Admirals also migrate and September is a good time to see them passing by. Migrating only to states farther south, some adults have even been known to survive a mild winter in the north."

Backyard Almanac

Life Cycle: One or two broods each year. Flight period from May to October. Adults may hibernate during mild winters, but more likely migrate.

Eggs: Greenish and barrel-shaped. Eggs laid on nettles.

Caterpillar: Black to yellowish-green with black and yellow stripes and blackish spines.

Chrysalis: Brown, gold-flecked with dull short tubercles on thorax and curved abdomen.

Cryptically-colored underwings are drab compared to the striking uppersides.

Wintering: Overwinters as chrysalis. May migrate or hibernate as an adult.

Caterpillar Food: Nettles, wood nettle, hops.

Adult Food: Red clover, alfalfa, bog laurel, bog rosemary, lilac, common milkweed, spreading dogbane, blazing-stars, spotted joe-pye weed, asters, staghorn sumac. Also tree sap, rotten fruit and animal droppings.

White Admiral *Limenitis arthemis arthemis*

MAY	JUNE	JULY	AUGUST	SEPTEMBER

Northern forests along watercourses and nearby open areas, trails, roads.

Nature Notes:

Hybrids between the northern White Admiral and the more southern Red-spotted Purple appear south of the North Woods in central Minnesota, southern Wisconsin and lower Michigan.

Larry's Phenology Records

June 12th is the average first sighting of the White Admiral around Duluth based on ten years of observation. The earliest record was June 7th.

Description: Wingspan is 3 to 3½ inches.

Dark (blue-black) wings with white bands forming a horseshoe-shape when viewed while wings spread.

Above: Blue-black wings with sharply delineated white bands on all four wings ↑. Red-orange spots on hindwing submargins.

Below: Colorful undersides. Dark brown wings with broad white band ↑ and red-orange spots along edges and at base of forewing and hindwing. Blue spots at margin.

Similar Species: Red-spotted Purple has all dark wings but no white bands. The margin pattern is the same, however. It is a southern subspecies and the White Admiral is the northern subspecies. Hybrids appear south of here in central Minnesota, southern Wisconsin, lower Michigan and southern New England.

The color theme of a broad white band is carried through to the undersides too.

"[The White Admiral] basks on the trunks of trees and feeds on light-colored forest flowers but has some other options for food as well. These include sap, rotting fruit, dung and even honeydew from aphids. These butterflies are also attracted to sweat and visit clothes hanging outside."

Backyard Almanac

Life Cycle: One or two broods (second may be partial). First flight period from late May to late July. Second may go until early September.

Eggs: Pale green, compressed and oval. Deposited on leaf tip of host plant.

Caterpillar: Mottled brown-green with white saddle and humped thorax.

Chrysalis: Cream-colored with enlarged wing cases and saddle.

Wintering: Caterpillars overwinter in leafy case on host plants.

Caterpillar Food: Usually leaves from birches, aspens, willows and cherries. Occasionally hawthorns, basswood and juneberries.

Adult Food: Takes in nutrients from mammal scat, bird guano, aphid honey, puddles, wet sand or pavement. Usually does not nectar on flowers but occasionally found on milkweeds and spotted joe-pye weed.

The more southern Red-spotted Purple subspecies appears south of the North Woods in central Minnesota, southern Wisconsin, lower Michigan and southern New England.

Viceroy *Limenitis archippus*

MAY	JUNE	JULY	AUGUST	SEPTEMBER

Open areas near water courses, wet areas with willows, swamps, marshes, damp meadows, lake margins, roadside ditches, and riversides.

Nature Notes:

Mimics the Monarch, but may also be distasteful to birds itself.

Caterpillars feed at night.

Second brood more likely to nectar.

Perch low and return to same sites after flights.

Description: Wingspan is 2½ to 3¼ inches.

Striking orange-and-black mimic of the Monarch.

Above: Orange with black veins and margins. Double row of white dots in black borders. Hindwing shows a distinct curved black line arcing across the postmedians ↑.

Below: Similar to above, but lighter.

Similar Species: The Monarch, whom it mimics is quite a bit larger and lacks the curved black postmedian lines.

Life Cycle: Two broods each year is normal. Flight period from early July to early September.

Eggs: Placed on tips of willow leaves (sandbar willow especially). The eggs may blend in with galls on leaves.

Note the connected black line on the underwing that helps separate the mimic Viceroy from the Monarch.

Caterpillar: Olive-green with blotches of white (saddle-patch) and a pair of spiny thoracic horns. Mature caterpillars appear mildly fearsome. Can look like bird droppings.

Chrysalis: Up to ⅞ inch. Brown and cream-colored, disk on back. Looks like a bird dropping.

Wintering: Overwinters as caterpillar in leaf-tip shelter.

Caterpillar Food: Leaves of willows: especially small shrubby species. Some apple, aspens, cherries and wild plums.

Adult Food: Asters, goldenrods, thistles, spotted joe-pye weed, blackberries, bouncing bet. Also takes moisture and nutrients from damp soil, carrion, dung, honey dew and fungi.

Northern Pearly-eye *Enodia anthedon*

MAY	JUNE	JULY	AUGUST	SEPTEMBER

Edges of deciduous woods; usually near streams, swamps.

Nature Notes:

Very territorial. Perch on tree trunks and fly out aggressively at passing butterflies.

May be active early a.m. or late p.m., when they court.

Named for the pearly-pupiled "eyes" found on the underside of its wings.

Living in the forests, adults forego nectar, feeding instead on sap from various trees, including willows, aspens and birches.

Description: Wingspan is 2 to 2½ inches.

The Northern Pearly-eye is one of the few butterflies we find in the woods in midsummer. Its tan wings marked with twenty or so "eyes" makes this butterfly quite noticeable. Orangish antennae with black and white tip.

Above: Tan with zigzag lines on forewing wrist ↑ and many dark eyespots; three on each forewing and five large ones on each hindwing ↑.

Below: Brown with a lavender tint. Several wavy lines and many eyespots with white pupils; four on each forewing encircled by a white band ↑. The white pupils of the eyespots are the "pearly eyes" it's named for. Postmedian line is relatively straight.

Similar Species: Eyed Brown is very similar but it is lighter brown above and below and with smaller eyespots. Also its postmedian line below is quite jagged. Little Wood-Satyr has fewer eyespots above and below.

"*Their eye-spots, best seen from the under-side, intimidate other critters by making the Northern Pearly-eyes appear aggressive.*"

Backyard Almanac

Many bold and large eyespots help distinguish this species from its cousin, the Eyed Brown.

Life Cycle: One brood. Hatch in fall. Flight period from late May to early September.

Eggs: Greenish-white and barrel-shaped. Laid singly on host plant.

Caterpillar: Yellow-green with green and yellow stripes. Red-tipped "horns" at ends.

Chrysalis: Glossy green to blue-green.

Wintering: Caterpillars overwinter.

Caterpillar Food: Grasses: shorthusk, white-grasses or satin-grasses.

Adult Food: Sap from willows, aspens and birches. Also visit carrion and scat for whatever nutrients they might pick up. May come to bait or clothes.

Eyed Brown *Satyrodes eurydice*

MAY	JUNE	JULY	AUGUST	SEPTEMBER

Open marshes, sedge meadows, cattail swamps, slow-moving streams, ditches.

Nature Notes:

Female is larger than male.

Never in large numbers or widespread but may be locally common.

Weak flight.

Description: Wingspan is 1½ to 2¼ inches. Light brown with eyespots.

Above: Forewing is light brown and has four or five eyespots. Hindwing is light brown with five dark eyespots; several with white "pupils" ↑.

Below: Forewing light brown with four or five eyespots with white pupils. Three wavy "scribbled" lines closer to body ↑. Hindwing is also light brown and is marked by six or seven eyespots with white pupils and encircled by light rings ↑. Also note the three wavy lines and a post median band that is more zigzag ↑.

Similar Species: Northern Pearly-eyes are noticeably darker with fewer eyespots above and larger ones below. Appalachian Brown has smaller black eyespots and fewer wavy lines

The satyrs, wood-nymphs and browns can be a confusing group of butterflies. Look for these field marks when trying to positively identify an Eyed Brown.

under hindwing. Little Wood-Satyr is darker above with fewer yet larger eyespots and few wavy lines below.

Life Cycle: One brood each summer. Flight period from early July to late August.

Eggs: Laid singly on, or near, sedges.

Caterpillar: Yellow-green with reddish lateral stripes. Green head with pair of reddish "horns".

Chrysalis: Dark green and striped with buff.

Wintering: Overwinters as a mature caterpillar.

Caterpillar Food: Sedges.

Adult Food: Plant sap and bird droppings. Nectar from swamp milkweed and spotted joe-pye weed.

Little Wood-Satyr *Megisto cymela*

| MAY | JUNE | JULY | AUGUST | SEPTEMBER |

Grassland-woodland interface; openings of deciduous forests, brushy old fields, meadows, streamsides.

Nature Notes:

Often has two periods of emergence separated by about three weeks (too close to be considered a different generation).

Caterpillars feed at night in the fall.

Adults bask spreadwing on ground or low in greenery.

They have a dancing, slow-motion flight.

Do well in fragmented forests.

Description: Wingspan is 1⅝ to 1⅞ inches.

Dark brown above with eight evenly spaced eyes. Light brown below.

Above: Two yellow-ringed black eyespots on both the forewing and hindwing ↑.

Below: Light brown (tan) with more prominent yellow-ringed black eyespots; silvery scales. Some eyespots could have double pupils. Note the two relatively straight lines crossing wings ↑.

Similar Species: Eyed Brown and Northern Pearly-eye are both larger with more numerous eyespots below and wavier underwing lines.

Life Cycle: One brood each summer. Flight period from late May to late July. Males peak in mid June. Females peak in late June.

Little Wood-Satyr on the ground possibly feeding on bird droppings.

Eggs: Yellow-green on various grasses.

Caterpillar: Pale brown and tinged with green. Medium black stripes and brown patches. Covered with fine hairs and small tubercles.

Chrysalis: Rounded with two brown stripes and two rows of brown dots on abdomen. Curved at rear towards point of attachment. Stuck on sedge stem.

Wintering: Overwinters as caterpillar.

Caterpillar Food: Grasses: orchard grass and Kentucky bluegrass.

Adult Food: Common milkweed, white sweet clover, ox-eye daisy, dewberry, staghorn sumac, viburnums. Sap, bird droppings and aphid honeydew.

Common Ringlet *Coenonympha tullia*

MAY	JUNE	JULY	AUGUST	SEPTEMBER

Low grassy fields, moist fields, marsh edges, meadows, road-sides, forest edges, prairies, bogs and sites where grass has been undisturbed for a few years.

Nature Notes:

Unlike other satyrs, Common Ringlets are frequent nectarers.

Jerky, bouncing flight just above the grass tops.

Only ringlet in the North Woods.

Range is expanding.

Highly variable in color and eyespots.

Female brighter than male.

Description: Wingspan is 1 to $1\frac{7}{8}$ inches.

Pale orange-brown. Orangish flash ↑ often visible when flying. Rarely rests with wings spread.

Above: Orange-brown to ochre-brown with few markings.

Below: Forewing shows orange-gray with one black eyespot ringed with yellow ↑. Hindwing is even brown-gray with a wavy partial white postmedian line ↑.

Similar Species: Little Wood-Satyr is a bit larger, much darker and with several clear eyespots. Red-disked Alpine is darker with no obvious underwing markings.

Life Cycle: One brood each summer. Flight period from early June to late July.

Eggs: Pale green and barrel-shaped.

Caterpillar: Dark green with pale green lateral line, white ventral band and green head with white papillae.

Chrysalis: Translucent green-brown with nine black stripes.

Wintering: Overwinters as caterpillar.

Caterpillar Food: Grasses. Some rushes.

Adult Food: Yellow hawkweed, alsike clover, fleabanes, mints.

Common Wood-Nymph *Cercyonis pegala*

MAY	JUNE	JULY	AUGUST	SEPTEMBER

Open brushy fields, prairies, woodland edges, roadsides, near slow-moving water, marshes.

Nature Notes:

Unlike other satyrs, nectars at flowers.

Males seldom feed.

Not found in the woods as its name would imply.

Highly variable in color.

Usually not seen spreadwing.

Description: Wingspan is 2 to 3 inches.

Dark with dull yellow forewing patches surrounding two eyespots. Northern populations may lack this patch. Female is larger, paler and with bigger eyespots.

Above: Dark brown with two black eyespots with white pupils on each forewing. Some forms have dull to light yellow patches surrounding the eyespots ↑. The "pegala" subspecies have these patches; "nephela" subspecies do not.

Below: Forewing undersides have two yellow-ringed eyespots with white pupils ↑. Hindwing with several (usually six) small eyespots with white pupils. Lighter and darker zones separated by a single dark line.

The lighter patch on the forewing undersides is visible even at great distances.

Similar Species: Northern Pearly-eye is not as dark and has more eyespots. Eyed Brown is lighter brown with smaller eyespots.

Life Cycle: One brood each summer. Flight period from late June to mid August. Males fly about two to three weeks. Females emerge later and fly about a month.

Eggs: Yellow. Deposited on various grass species.

Caterpillar: Pale green with pale yellow stripe and reddish forked tail.

Chrysalis: green and plump.

Wintering: Overwinters as a caterpillar.

Caterpillar Food: Grasses: big bluestem.

Adult Food: Alfalfa, mints, meadowsweet, blue vervain, wild bergamot, milkweeds, asters, fleabanes, spotted knapweed, goldenrods, spotted joe-pye weed, sunflowers. Also rotting fruit and sap.

Jutta Arctic *Oeneis jutta*

MAY	JUNE	JULY	AUGUST	SEPTEMBER

Black spruce and tamarack bogs.

Nature Notes:

A northern butterfly that is very at home in the bogs.

Adults frequently found resting on trunks of spruce or tamarack.

Description: Wingspan is 1½ to 2 inches.

Above: Dull gray-brown with yellow submargin. Forewing with one to four black spots. One or two spots on hindwing.

Below: Large subapical eyespot on forewing surrounded by tawny ring ↑. Hindwing shows shades of gray-black; looking like bark.

Similar Species: Hindwing of Macoun's Arctic is darker below; white eyespot on forewing. Chryxus Arctic is lighter below with a small white eyespot.

Life Cycle: Single-brooded. Flight period from early June to mid July. Biennial (takes two years to complete life cycle).

Jutta Arctics are at home in the black spruce and tamarack bogs of the northern U.S.

Eggs: White and barrel-shaped. Laid on cotton-grass.

Caterpillar: Pale green with brownish lateral line and reddish hairs; green head.

Chrysalis: Yellow-green with green wing cases; brown abdomen markings and amber head.

Wintering: Overwinters as a caterpillar. First year of life cycle as young larva; second year winters over as mature larva.

Caterpillar Food: Cotton-grasses, sedges, rushes.

Adult Food: Labrador tea.

Monarch   *Danaus plexippus (male left and female right)*

MAY	JUNE	JULY	AUGUST	SEPTEMBER

Open fields, roadsides, suburban areas, disturbed ground.

Nature Notes:

During the fall migration of September and October, Monarchs may assemble in large numbers on foliage along lake shores.

Overwinter as adults in huge concentrations in Sierra Madre Mountains of central Mexico. Up to 20 million may gather there.

Most caterpillars and adults are distasteful due to ingestion of milkweeds.

Larry's Phenology Records

May 19th is the earliest I have encountered a northbound migrant. The ten-year average first date of arrival is May 29th.

Description: Wingspan is 3½ to 4½ inches.

Orange, with striking pattern of black. White dots in black border. Four walking legs. A very large butterfly.

Above: Orange with prominent black veins and borders. Males have a small black oval-shaped scent patch on each hindwing ↑.

Below: As above, only a little paler.

Similar Species: Viceroy, the well known Monarch-mimic is smaller with a solid black line crossing the hindwing. Great Spangled Fritillary is slightly smaller with orange and black spots, chevrons and zig-zigs.

Life Cycle: Two broods each year in the north. Arrival from the south (around June 1st); caterpillars by June 20th; pupation by early July; next-generation larvae by August 15th which pupate in late August. Flight period from late May to late September. (See pages 6 and 7.)

Eggs: Pale green and shaped like lemons. Placed singly under milkweed leaves.

Lack of the oval black scent patch means this is a female Monarch.

"Paper-thin but very durable wings carry them on this one-way journey. Hundreds of miles to the south, the Monarchs will winter in high altitude fir trees in the Sierra Madre mountains in central Mexico. Congregating flocks are so numerous that they turn the ever-green branches orange."

Backyard Almanac

Caterpillar: Banded black, yellow and white. Head is black and white. Pair of black filaments at both the front and rear ends. Up to two-inches long. Live two weeks as a caterpillar.

Chrysalis: Nearly one-inch long. Pale green and flecked with glistening gold. Rounded lid. About one week in this pupal stage.

Wintering: Migrate south throughout our area from August to September. Overwinter as adults in the Sierra Madre mountains of central Mexico. In the very early spring they begin to move north, stopping to lay eggs in Texas. Next generation migrates north arriving in the North Woods in late May to early June.

Caterpillar Food: Milkweeds; especially common milkweed.

Adult Food: Milkweeds, spreading dogbane, red clover, Labrador tea, lilac, goldenrods, spotted knapweed, thistles, spotted joe-pye weed, asters, sunflowers.

A mature Monarch caterpillar on its favorite food plant—common milkweed.

Silver-spotted Skipper

Arctic Skipper

Long Dash

Dreamy Duskywing

European Skipper

Skippers
Family Hesperiidae

Up to 3500 species worldwide. Mostly tropical, but about 280 species in North America. Rapid darting flight gives them their common name. These small butterflies have relatively large bodies compared to wing size. Antennae are hooked and clubbed with a pointed apicular. Most are drab and many males have scent scales (stigma) on the forewings. All six legs are fully developed. Eyes are large, proboscis is long and they take nectar. Many also go to rotting material or mud. Basking is done with forewings vertical and hindwings spread flat.

The globular eggs are placed singly on host plants. The tapered green caterpillars feed at night. Chrysalis are smooth and long. Overwinter as a caterpillar or chrysalis.

Spread-winged Skippers (Subfamily Pyrginae)

They often bask with open wings. Adults take nectar, but males also go to wet sand or mud. Most are dark (gray or brown), some with white spots or bands. Largest of the skippers. Antennae are curved, banana-shaped, with an angled apicular. Eggs laid on host plants. Caterpillars feed at night on oaks and legumes. They stay in rolled leaves in a webbed shelter where they also overwinter.

Grass Skippers (Subfamily Hesperiinae)

Large group with more than 200 species in North America. Most are small, usually less than an inch long. They have angled antennae with an apicular. Front wings of males often with a brand or stigma (specialized cells). Many are orange or brown and males and females are often differently colored (sexual dimorphism). When basking, they hold the front wings nearly vertical and the hindwings horizontal. Only the Arctic Skipper basks with wings completely spread. They have a rapid flight. With a long proboscis, they nectar frequently, but some go to sand and mud. Caterpillars feed on grasses at night within a silken shelter. They overwinter as caterpillars.

Silver-spotted Skipper *Epargyreus clarus*

MAY	JUNE	JULY	AUGUST	SEPTEMBER

Woodlands bordered by openings; riparian forests, streamsides, roadsides, parks, suburbs, brushy areas, fields, meadows, gardens.

Nature Notes:

Caterpillars hide during the day.

Adults roost upside down.

Description: Wingspan is 1¾ to 2½ inches.

Dark with large light-colored stripes. A large skipper with very pointed wings. Wings are spread at rest.

Above: Dark brown with semitransparent yellowish rectangular spots on pointed forewing ↑. Hindwings sport slight tail-like projections.

Below: Forewing is much like the upper forewing. The underside of the hindwing presents the large diagnostic irregularly-shaped silver spot ↑.

Similar Species: None. This is the largest skipper in our area.

Life Cycle: One brood each summer. Flight period from late June to mid August.

The large, irregular-shaped silver spot is diagnostic of this species.

Eggs: Green and globular. Placed on plants of the pea family.

Caterpillar: Yellow with greenish lines. Brown head with two large orange spots. Mature caterpillars form feeding shelters in leaves of host plants.

Chrysalis: Dark brown and formed in leafy shelters at base of host plants.

Wintering: Caterpillar overwinters.

Caterpillar Food: Legumes: including beggar's-ticks, wild peas, hog-peanut.

Adult Food: Alfalfa, vetches, red clover, blackberries, wild bergamot, honeysuckles, staghorn sumac, New Jersey tea, self-heal, purple loosestrife, spreading dogbane, common milkweed, swamp milkweed, spotted knapweed, black-eyed susan, blazing-stars, fleabanes, thistles, wild iris.

Northern Cloudywing *Thorybes pylades*

| MAY | JUNE | JULY | AUGUST | SEPTEMBER |

Open areas, powerline cuts, forest edges, moist meadows, brushy fields, roadsides, often where quack-grasses grow.

Nature Notes:

More boreal than other cloudywings and the most widespread.

Perches on or near the ground in clearings.

Will go to mud puddles.

Swift flight.

Prefers to nectar on blue, purple or pink flowers.

Description: Wingspan is 1¼ to 1¾ inches.

Evenly brown to dark gray, including the face. A large skipper.

Above: Evenly brown with two thin triangular white flecks on outer forewing ↑.

Below: Much like above. Brown band on hindwing and frosted gray on outer edges.

Similar Species: Duskywings are also dark, but more gray and no, or very few, white spots on forewings above.

Life Cycle: One brood each summer. Flight period from late May to early July, peaking in June.

Eggs: Light green, turning white before hatching. Placed on legumes.

The underside of a Northern Cloudywing is
very similar to its topside.

Caterpillar: Dark green with brownish dorsal
and orange-pink lateral lines; short hairs. Head
is black to dark brown.

Chrysalis: Dark brown, tan and olive mottled
with black.

Wintering: Overwinters as caterpillar in leaf-
shelter.

Caterpillar Food: Legumes: including clovers,
alfalfa, wild-peas and milk-vetches.

Adult Food: Prefers pink, blue or purple flowers. Not likely to nectar on flowers of yellow,
orange or red. Downy phlox, self heal, blueberries, spreading dogbane, common milkweed,
purple vetch, red clover, alfalfa, crown vetch,
thistles.

Dreamy Duskywing *Erynnis icelus*

MAY	JUNE	JULY	AUGUST	SEPTEMBER

Open woodlands, damp areas with willows, cut-over forests, brushy fields, bogs, roadsides, trails.

Nature Notes:

Found further north than the Sleepy Duskywing.

Duskywings are very difficult to separate in the field.

Description: Wingspan is 1 to 1⅜ inches.

Dark with gray patches on forewing. Light spots on hindwing.

Above: Chain-like postmedian band ↑ on grizzled brown forewing. Gray patch along "wrist" ↑. Small white dot near this band and patch. Hindwing is dark with submarginal light spots.

Below: Both forewing and hindwing are dark with submarginal light spots.

Similar Species: Sleepy Duskywing's forewing patch is more brown with no white dot. It is also larger. Juvenal's Duskywing has a darker center. Forewing has smaller gray patch and no postmedian band.

Life Cycle: One brood each summer. Flight period from early May to early July.

Dreamy Duskywing is a beautiful name for a butterfly. Both the Dreamy and Sleepy Duskywings have pale spots on their undersides.

Eggs: Column-shaped and pale green.

Caterpillar: Pale green with small white scattered bumps with hairs. Black head is angular with reddish and yellowish spots. Makes nest of leaves tied together with silk.

Chrysalis: Brown or green.

Wintering: Overwinters as a caterpillar in leaf shelters.

Caterpillar Food: Willows, aspens and maybe birches.

Adult Food: Blossoms of blackberries, blueberries, cherries and wild strawberries. Also Labrador tea, New Jersey tea, bog laurel, hoary puccoon, winter-cresses, alsike clover, purple vetch, lupines, spreading dogbane, ox-eye daisy. Newly emerged males take moisture from damp soil on dirt roads.

Juvenal's Duskywing *Erynnis juvenalis (female)*

MAY	JUNE	JULY	AUGUST	SEPTEMBER

Oak woodlands, edges, paths, openings; adjacent fields, cut-over forests.

Nature Notes:

Common and wide-spread.

Males are territorial and aggressive.

Sleeps with wings folded roof-like over body as many moths do.

Spreadwing basking is done on the ground or on limbs of shrubs.

Description: Wingspan is 1¼ to 1¾ inches.

Males are an even dark brown, almost black. Females paler and patterned (pictured above).

Above: Male forewing is dark with black bands and chevrons. Triangular mark on forewing tip ↑. Plain long hairs on hindwing. Female similar but lighter and more patterned.

Below: Forewing similar to above. Hindwing undersides have two small round light spots near apex ↑.

Similar Species: Northern Cloudywing is an unpatterned brown color with white spots on the forewing. Dreamy Duskywing has a chain-like postmedian band on the upper forewing and a gray patch on the "wrist". Sleepy Duskywing has more white spots on the upper hindwing.

Juvenal's Duskywing almost always shows two white spots on the underside of the hindwings.

Life Cycle: One brood each summer. Flight period from mid May to early July.

Eggs: Green; turning pink. Laid on oaks.

Caterpillar: Blue-green or dark green. Body with tiny yellow-white dots. Head is tan to green-brown with four orange spots.

Chrysalis: Dark green to brown.

Wintering: Overwinters as caterpillar.

Caterpillar Food: Oaks; especially northern red oak.

Adult Food: Alfalfa, blackberries, blueberries, chokecherry, wild strawberries, wild plum, lilac, honeysuckles, lupines. Goes for moisture and minerals at damp soils.

Arctic Skipper *Carterocephalus palaemon*

MAY	JUNE	JULY	AUGUST	SEPTEMBER

Moist grassy open areas near oak-pine forests, stream margins, bogs, swamps, sedge lowlands.

Nature Notes:

A northern butterfly, circumpolar, but not restricted to the arctic.

Mating behavior includes a display where males and females open and close their wings in unison.

Description: Wingspan is 1 to 1¼ inches.

Bright and attractive northern skipper. Checkered orange and brown.

Above: Very dark brown and dabbed with large, evenly-spaced orange spots.

Below: Large white spots on orange-brown background ↑. Forewing shows dark spots on yellow-orange. Hindwing has large white spots on orange background.

Similar Species: Peck's Skipper's light patches are longer, square and not white. No other skipper of this color will spread its wings while basking.

Life Cycle: One brood. Caterpillars overwinter. Flight period from late May to mid July.

Left. Arctic Skippers bask with their wings open more than others in this family.
Below. A pair of mating skippers. Courtship behavior involves simultaneous wing-spreading.

Eggs: Greenish-white.

Caterpillar: Creamy to blue-green with green dorsal stripes, yellow lateral stripes and black spots below. Whitish head.

Chrysalis: Looks like a fragment of faded grass.

Wintering: Caterpillar overwinters.

Caterpillar Food: Grasses: purple reedgrass or brome-grass.

Adult Food: Labrador tea, wild iris, bog laurel.

European Skipper *Thymelicus lineola*

MAY	JUNE	JULY	AUGUST	SEPTEMBER

Dry grassy fields, especially with tall grasses, pastures, parks, roadsides, railways, marshes, bog edges, forest clearings.

Nature Notes:

Introduced into London, Ontario in 1910. Recorded for the first time in the United States in 1925.

Range is still expanding.

May be transported in bales of timothy.

Thousands of individuals have been recorded on single day counts for the North American Butterfly Association's Fourth of July survey.

Roost at night by the hundreds on grassy stalks.

Description: Wingspan is ¾ to 1 inch.

Mostly orange with black wing borders. Short reddish antennae with blunt clubs.

Above: Orange with a narrow black border ↑. Veins lined with black. Male with a thin black stigma on forewing.

Below: Light orange without distinguishing marks. Forewing is solid orange while hindwing is more olive-ochre.

Similar Species: The Least Skipper is smaller more black above and brighter orange below. Black and white antennae instead of red. Delaware Skipper is larger with wider black margins above. Also, they have no stigma and a longer, hooked antenna.

Life Cycle: One brood each summer. Flight period from mid June to early August, peaking in July.

Eggs: Whitish. Deposited in groups of 30 to 40 on grasses; especially timothy.

Caterpillar: Green with a dark dorsal stripe. Head is light brown with white or yellow stripes.

Chrysalis: Yellow-green with down-curved horns.

Wintering: Overwinters as eggs.

Caterpillar Food: Grasses, especially timothy and sometimes quack-grasses.

Adult Food: Red clover, alsike clover, vetches, spreading dogbane, common milkweed, swamp milkweed, pepper-grass, New Jersey tea, mints, self-heal, ox-eye daisy, orange hawkweed, yellow hawkweed, black-eyed susan, fleabanes, thistles.

Hundreds of European Skippers puddling on a wet dirt road taking in moisture and nutrients. This can be a fairly common sight in rural areas in July.

Like its name implies, this butterfly is originally a European species. It was introduced into Canada in the early 1900s.

Indian Skipper   *Hesperia sassacus*

| MAY | JUNE | JULY | AUGUST | SEPTEMBER |

Brushy fields, open meadows near woodlands, clearings, pastures.

Nature Notes:

May be widespread and locally common, but never abundant.

A northern skipper.

Description: Wingspan is 1 to 1¼ inches. Mostly orange-black.

Above: Forewing is orange with black borders and a black stigma (males) ↑. Hindwing is orange with well-defined black border.

Below: Forewing is yellow-orange with brown border. Hindwing has light-colored rectangles that form a "V" ↑ (more pronounced in females).

Similar Species: Hobomok Skipper's undersides have larger yellow patches. The Long Dash is much darker above and its hindwing below shows the rectangular patches more clearly.

An Indian Skipper takes up moisture from a patch of wet sand. The
black stigma ↑ proves that this is a male.

Life Cycle: Single brooded. Flight period from
early June to mid July.

Eggs: Round and white. Laid on grasses.

Caterpillar: Olive-green with a black head.
Lives in a silken shelter at the base of grasses.
Caterpillar leaves shelter to feed.

Chrysalis: Various shades of brown.

Wintering: Overwinters as caterpillar.

Caterpillar Food: Grasses: panic grasses, big
bluestem, red fescue.

Adult Food: Blackberries, honeysuckles,
Labrador tea, wild iris, hoary puccoon, red
clover, vetches, ox-eye daisy, orange hawkweed.

Peck's Skipper *Polites peckius*

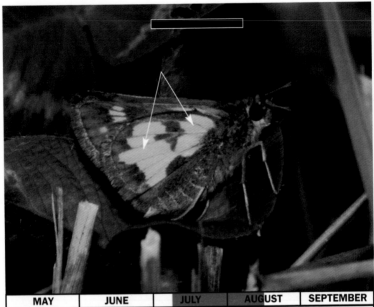

MAY	JUNE	JULY	AUGUST	SEPTEMBER

Any open grassy areas; meadows, lawns, parks, pastures, vacant lots, suburbs, old fields, powerline cuts, forest clearings, marshes.

Nature Notes:

One of the most common skippers in the east.

Formerly known as the "Yellowpatch Skipper."

Description: Wingspan is ¾ to 1¼ inches.

Black-orange above and two-toned orange below.

Above: Forewing is dark with orange costal area and orange rectangular spots beyond stigma (male). Hindwing is dark with orange marks in the shape of an "X" ↑. Remember, "Peck's has the X".

Below: Forewing is orange-black, darker towards base, lighter towards submargin. Hindwing marked by large blotches of light orange ↑ on darker orange background including a very long light-colored bar.

Similar Species: Hobomok Skipper lacks the light-colored patch at the base of the hindwing below. Long Dash is more orange above in males and shows smaller light-colored patches

Note the X-shaped mark on the hindwing's topside. Remember, "Peck's has the X".

on the hindwing below.

Life Cycle: One brood each summer. Flight period from early July to mid August.

Eggs: Green and spherical. Found on several species of grasses.

Caterpillar: Maroon with light brown mottling. Head is black with white markings.

Chrysalis: Maroon with white appendage cases.

Wintering: Overwinters as caterpillar.

Caterpillar Food: Grasses.

Adult Food: Red clover, vetches, alfalfa, spreading dogbane, common milkweed, swamp milkweed, wild iris, downy phlox, New Jersey tea, self-heal, blue vervain, blazing-stars.

Tawny-edged Skipper *Polites themistocles*

MAY	JUNE	JULY	AUGUST	SEPTEMBER

Open grassy areas; meadows, old fields, pastures, disturbed areas, yards, gardens, vacant lots, forest openings, roadsides.

Nature Notes:

Widespread through much of the United States and Canada. One of the most widespread of all skippers.

More common in the east.

Description: Wingspan is ³/₄ to 1¹/₄ inches.

Mostly dull olive with tawny-orange on leading edge of forewing ↑.

Above: Male forewing has an orange front half (costal area), but mostly olive-brown with thick black stigma. Rectangular orange patch at end of stigma. Female forewing has a more subtle costal mark and three or four orange spots. Hindwing of both is dark.

Below: Forewing is light gray-brown with orange costal areas. Hindwing is drab orange-brown to mustard color.

Similar Species: Crossline Skipper has a thinner and straighter stigma with pale yellow spots adjacent to it. Hindwing has a light post-median spot-band below. It is also larger.

Life Cycle: Single brood. Flight period from mid June to early August.

Eggs: Pale greenish. Laid on panic grasses.

Caterpillar: Dark brown with mottling and a blackish head. Two white vertical stripes at front.

Chrysalis: Dull white, green and brown.

Wintering: Overwinters as caterpillar or chrysalis.

Caterpillar Food: Grasses: panic grasses, Kentucky bluegrass, crab-grasses.

Adult Food: Alfalfa, red clover, sweetclovers, vetches, spreading dogbane, ox-eye daisy, orange hawkweed, spotted knapweed, thistles. Some take moisture from damp areas along country roads.

Long Dash *Polites mystic*

MAY	JUNE	JULY	AUGUST	SEPTEMBER

Wet meadows, wetlands, along streams, marshes (often with wild iris). Drier sites further north; forest edges, abandoned fields, roads.

Nature Notes:

Northern skipper.

Adapted to farmed areas.

Perches on low sites in the sun.

Named Long Dash because of the long black stigma on the male's wings.

Description: Wingspan is 1 to 1¼ inches.

Orange and black. Note the male's angled black "dash" on the forewings that is actually the stigma.

Above: Male has orange wings with wide black borders. Wide black marking (stigma) ↑ in center of forewing dividing the orange. Stigma joins another black dash causing it to appear longer (hence the name "long dash"). Female has darker wings with less orange.

Below: Male is yellow-brown with a light, crescent-shaped postmedian band made up of equal-sized yellow rectangles ↑. Female shows a wide yellow-orange band and scattered spots.

Similar Species: Indian Skipper has a thinner stigma. It is more orange above and paler below. Peck's Skipper's stigma is not as wide; less orange above. Also remember that "Peck's has the X" on the underwing.

Most skippers are quite tiny. Compare the size of this Long Dash with the finger it sits on.

Life Cycle: One brood each summer. Flight period from mid June to early August.

Eggs: Deposited on Kentucky bluegrass and other grasses.

Caterpillar: Dark brown with white mottling and a black head; short spines.

Chrysalis: Formed in early spring on grasses.

Wintering: Overwinters as caterpillar.

Caterpillar Food: Grasses: Kentucky bluegrass, barnyard-grass, quack-grasses, timothy.

Adult Food: Wild iris, blackberry, red clover, lupines, alfalfa, white sweet clover, yellow sweet clover, vetches, self-heal, common milkweed, fleabanes, orange hawkweed, thistles.

Northern Broken-Dash   *Wallengrenia egeremet*

| MAY | JUNE | JULY | AUGUST | SEPTEMBER |

Open fields, meadows, brushy fields, pastures, forest edges, gardens, roadsides.

Nature Notes:

Often hard to distinguish between Northern Broken-Dash, Little Glassywing and Dun Skipper.

Name comes from the two-parted stigma on male's forewing.

Even though it is called the Northern Broken-Dash, it is mainly a southern skipper.

Description: Wingspan is 1 to 1¼ inches.

Mostly dark.

Above: Male forewing is dark with a rectangular orange spot ↑ at end of the two-parted stigma ↑. Female forewing bands with rectangular pale spot. Hindwing is all dark.

Below: Forewing is dark with light sub-apex spot. Hindwing is dark with a faint postmedian band in the shape of a backwards "3" ↑.

Similar Species: Dun Skipper is even darker with spots and shows no orange. Hobomok Skipper female is dark but with smaller white spots below on the forewing. Little Glassywing does not have orange above and the postmedian band below on the hindwing is straight.

This Northern Broken-Dash is nectaring at a blooming common milkweed; probably the most important late summer nectar source in the North Woods.

Life Cycle: One brood each summer. Flight period from late June to mid August.

Eggs: Pale green or yellow-white and round. Laid on panic grasses.

Caterpillar: Pale mottled green with indistinct green and yellow lateral stripes. Dark brown head with dark and light stripes.

Chrysalis: Green. Brownish on head; yellow-green on abdomen.

Wintering: Overwinters as caterpillar.

Caterpillar Food: Panic grasses.

Adult Food: Alfalfa, red clover, vetches, New Jersey tea, common milkweed, spreading dogbane, blazing-stars.

Hobomok Skipper *Poanes hobomok*

| MAY | JUNE | JULY | AUGUST | SEPTEMBER |

Woodland paths, edges, openings, fields, meadows, roadsides.

Nature Notes:

Most butterflies bask in the sun with wings held open or flat. Others hold their wings parallel over their back and place themselves broadside to the sun. The skippers combine these two techniques and hold their forewings vertical over their back while the hindwings stay horizontal. You can see this in many of the skipper photos in this book.

Description: Wingspan is 1 to 1½ inches.

Orange and dark brown-black.

Above: Male is yellow-orange with a wide brown border ↑ and dark veins. Short black stigma is low on wings. "Pocahontas" form of female is all dark with several tiny white dots.

Below: Large pale patches on hindwing ↑. Brown (purple-gray) cast to the wide trailing edge borders ↑. Brown at base of hindwing. Purple-brown wings with white-cream spots on forewing.

Similar Species: Peck's Skipper shows more underside orange including an area at the base of the wing. Above, it is less orange.

Skippers have large bodies relative to their wing size.

Life cycle: A single brood in the summer. Flight period from late May to mid July.

Eggs: Pale green. Laid singly on grasses.

Caterpillar: Dark green to brown with small black tubercles and spines.

Chrysalis: Reddish-brown with brown markings.

Wintering: Overwinters as chrysalis.

Caterpillar Food: Grasses: Kentucky bluegrass and panic grasses.

Adult Food: Blackberries, honeysuckles, lilac, Labrador tea, red clover, vetches, wild iris, milkweeds, downy phlox, wild strawberry, dandelion, orange hawkweed.

Dun Skipper *Euphyes vestris (female)*

MAY	JUNE	JULY	AUGUST	SEPTEMBER

Moist open sites near deciduous woods or meadows.
Roadsides, disturbed areas, powerline cuts, streamsides.

Nature Notes:

Often on damp soil and leaves. Males take moisture and nutrients from soil, carrion and dung.

Swift flight.

Perches on low shrubs.

Description: Wingspan is 1 to 1¼ inches.

Whole body dark with triangular wings. Male's head is yellowish-gold.

Above: Brownish black. Male is all dark with black stigma on forewing. Female with two tiny yellow-white spots on forewing ↑.

Below: Dark and unmarked. Male with pale lavender border on the hindwing. Female has a faint yellow band on hindwing.

Similar Species: Northern Broken-Dash female is not as dark and has two elongated yellow-orange spots on forewing and longer white dashes. Male shows some orange. Female Hobomok Skipper (Pocahontas form) has more white markings above and below.

Dun Skipper nectaring on spotted knapweed. Note the unmarked underwings.

Life Cycle: One brood each summer. Flight period from late June to mid August.

Eggs: Pale green turning reddish on top. Placed singly on sedges.

Caterpillar: Light green with white dashes. Head is black, brown and cream.

Chrysalis: Blunt and ridged. Various shades of green, yellow and brown.

Wintering: Overwinters as partially grown caterpillar.

Caterpillar Food: Sedges.

Adult Food: Red clover, vetches, fireweed, mints, wild bergamot, self-heal, spreading dogbane, common milkweed, spotted knapweed, blazing-stars, pussy-toes, thistles.

Pepper and Salt Skipper *Amblyscirtes hegon*

MAY	JUNE	JULY	AUGUST	SEPTEMBER

Edges and openings of mixed woods, paths, forest roads, grass-lined water courses. swamp edges, hay fields.

Nature Notes:

Gets its name from the speckled undersides.

Description: Wingspan is ¾ to 1 inch.

Gray with white spots.

Above: Forewing is dark gray with white spots tinged with yellow in shape of a "U" ↑. Hindwing is dark gray with a pale light-colored band.

Below: Both wings are grizzled "salt-and-pepper" gray ↑. Forewing shows a medial light-colored band and a checkered black-and-white trailing edge. Hindwing has a cream-colored postmedian band, tinged with yellow.

Similar Species: Both the Common Roadside-Skipper and the Dun Skipper are darker and show no checkered trailing edge.

Life Cycle: One brood each summer. Flight period from late May to late June.

The grizzled coloration of this skipper's underwings has led to its common name; Pepper and Salt Skipper.

Eggs: White and mostly placed on Indian grass and Kentucky bluegrass.

Caterpillar: Pale greenish-white with three dark green dorsal and two white lateral stripes. Head is dark brown with pale brown bands.

Chrysalis: Straw-colored with a green tinge.

Wintering: Overwinters as caterpillar.

Caterpillar Food: Grasses: Indian grass, Kentucky bluegrass.

Adult Food: Blackberries, blueberries, honeysuckles, lilac, viburnum, Virginia waterleaf, selfheal, spreading dogbane, white clover.

Day-Flying Moths: Butterfly Imposters

Nearly 95 percent of the order Lepidoptera are moths with only 5 percent being butterflies. Despite the huge numbers of moths, most are easy to distinguish from the butterflies. Moths usually have feathery or bushy antennae and fly at night. But with such a large and diverse group, it is understandable that a few moths can be confused with butterflies. Some are colorful. Some have thin antennae. Some are day-flyers. The following three are common in the North Woods. Don't let these butterfly imposters fool you.

Eight-spotted Forester *(Alypia octamaculata)*

Family Noctuidae

Wingspan is 1 to 1½ inches.

Description: Body is black. Wings are black with large oval spots. Forewings show pale yellow spots near body and two prominent white spots. Hindwing, like forewing, boldly spotted with white. Body is striped black and white.

Antennae are thin with thickened ends.

Adults visit flowers in open areas near streams and forests.

Peak flight period is May and June.

Spear-marked Black Moth *(Rheumaptera subhastata)*

Family Geometridae

Wingspan is 1 to 1½ inches.

Description: Body is dark. Wings are black with wide white bands. Forewings sport a broad white band. Hindwing has a narrow white band.

Antennae are thin and long.

Adults visit flowers in open sites near forests or swamps.

Peak flight period is June through July.

Virginia Ctenuchid *(Ctenucha virginica)*

Family Ctenuchidae

Wingspan is 1½ to 2 inches.

Description: Body is an iridescent blue with orange markings. Forewing is brownish-chestnut. Hindwings are usually covered as this butterfly imposter rarely rests in the spreadwing position.

Antennae are feathery.

Adults take nectar from flowers in open fields and marshes.

Peak flight period is May into July.

Eight-spotted Forester resting on a tarp. Thin antennae look more like those of a butterfly than a moth.

Above. Spear-marked Black Moths fly during the day and can confuse even veteran butterfly watchers.

Below. Virginia Ctenuchids are often found nectaring during daylight hours.

Glossary

Abdomen: The most posterior of the three main body parts.

Androconia: Specialized wing scales of males that produce odors used in courtship.

Antenna: One of a pair of long slender sensory appendages attached to the head (plural; antennae).

Anterior: Front part of the body; located near the head.

Apex: The tip of the forewing.

Apical: At the tip, or the area near the tip, of the forewing.

Apiculus: The slender portion of the antenna beyond the club. Found on some skippers.

Basal: The wing area near the body.

Basking: When a butterfly exposes its wings to sunlight in order to raise its temperature.

Bog: Wetland of acidic soil and sphagnum moss with some specialized plants.

Boreal: Refers to the northern coniferous forest region.

Cell: A relatively large central area of the wing enclosed by veins.

Chevron: A V-shaped pattern.

Chrysalis: The pupa stage of butterfly growth and metamorphosis.

Circumpolar: Occurring around the globe at northerly latitudes.

Claspers: Abdominal appendages on males used to hold females during mating.

Clubbed Antennae: Antennae that are thickened toward the end; not pointed.

Colonial: Living in groups or large populations. This may also include butterflies that establish temporary or permanent populations in a new area.

Composite: A plant composed of many small flowers in one blossom; Asteraceae is the family of these flowers. Important butterfly food source.

Costa: The upper or leading edge of the wing.

Cremaster: Hook-bearing structure at end of chrysalis; used as an attachment.

Diapause: A resting state in which bodily functions are minimized and energy is conserved.

Discal: The more central area of the wing.

Distal: Away from the body center.

Dorsal: The upper surface of the wing or the top side of a caterpillar.

Estivation: Dormancy or diapause during the summer or periods of hot weather.

Eyespot: A pattern of scales on a butterfly's wing resembling an eye.

Flight: In butterflies, a brood or generation.

Frenulum: A series of hooks that hold a moth's forewing and hindwing together in flight; not found on butterfly wings.

Forewings: The front or leading pair of wings.

Generation: From any given stage in a life cycle to the same stage in the offspring.

Genitalia: Sexual organs and associated structures.

Hibernaculum: A shelter in which the larva spends the winter.

Hibernation: Dormancy or diapause during winter; overwintering.

Hindwings: The rear pair of wings.

Host Plant: The specific food of a caterpillar.

Host-Specific: Restricted to a single plant or group of plants as a source of food.

Instar: One of several stages of caterpillar growth.

Larva: Caterpillar. The immature stage between the egg and the pupa (chrysalis); (plural; larvae).

Lateral: Referring to the side of an organism's body.

Leading Margin: The margin of the hindwing that is on top as the butterfly sits upright.

Lepidoptera: The order of insects containing butterflies and moths. "Scale-winged" in Latin.

Margin: The edge of the wing.

Medial/Median: The middle of the wing.

Metamorphosis: Changes in form occurring during the life cycle; butterflies change from larva (caterpillar) to pupa (chrysalis) to adult.

Migration: A regular two-way movement to and from wintering or breeding ranges.

Nectar: The sugary fluid secreted by flowers of many plants. The principal food for many adult butterflies.

Oblique: Having a slanting or sloping direction; inclined.

Osmeterium: A fleshy, tubular, Y-shaped scent gland at the head end of certain caterpillars.

Outer Angle: The area of the hindwing where the outer and trailing margins meet. The posterior region of the hindwing.

Outer Margin: The wing edge farthest from the body.

Overwinter: How butterflies spend winter; hibernate or diapause.

Oviposition: The act of egg laying; to oviposit.

Palpus: The two appendages on each side of the proboscis. (plural; palpi).

Papillae: Small, nipple-like projections.

Pheromone: Sex-attractant scent chemicals produced in scales of certain butterflies.

Polymorphism: The occurrence of several distinct forms within a species; sexual or seasonal.

Posterior: Located towards the rear; on or near the tail end.

Postmedial/Postmedian: Part of the wing just beyond the center or median.

Proboscis: The elongated extendible tube-like tongue of a butterfly; used to take in nectar, sap and minerals. Coiled when not in use.

Prolegs: The five pair of leg-like appendages on abdomen of caterpillar; false legs.

Pupa: In butterflies, the stage of the life cycle occurring between caterpillar (larva) and adult; the chrysalis.

Pupil: A spot near the center of an eyespot.

Scent Scales: Specialized scales for producing and dispersing pheromones; androconia.

Sexual Dimorphism: Two distinct forms of male and female of some butterflies.

Species: A group of individuals or populations that are similar in structure and physiology and are capable of interbreeding to produce fertile offspring.

Spiracles: Oval-shaped breathing vents along the sides of larvae or adult butterflies.

Stigma: An area of scent scales found on the forewings of some male skippers and hairstreaks (plural; stigmata).

Subapical: Referring to the region just before the tip of the wing.

Submarginal: Just within the outer wing margin.

Subspecies: A subdivision of a species; usually a geographic race. May appear different but is capable of interbreeding with others of the same species.

Tarsus: The terminal end of a butterfly's leg that is composed of several segments and contains chemoreceptors for smell (plural; tarsi).

Thorax: The portion of the body between the head and the abdomen.

Trailing Margin: Posterior, or rear, edge of the hindwing.

Tubercle: A raised, wartlike projection on some caterpillars which may contain spines.

Veins: A series of visibly raised structural elements on the wings which serve as struts.

Ventral: Referring to the underside of a butterfly's wing; underside of a caterpillar.

Appendix A
Checklist of North Woods Butterflies

Swallowtails (Family Papilionidae)
Swallowtails (Subfamily Papiloninae)
❏ Black Swallowtail   *Papilio polyxenes*
❏ Canadian Tiger Swallowtail   *Papilio canadensis*

Whites, Marbles & Sulphurs (Family Pieridae)
Whites (Subfamily Pierinae)
❏ Checkered White   *Pontia protodice*
❏ Western White   *Pontia occidentalis*
❏ Mustard White   *Pieris napi*
❏ Cabbage White   *Pieris rapae*
❏ West Virginia White   *Pieris virginiensis*
❏ Olympia Marble   *Euchloe olympia*
❏ Large Marble   *Euchloe ausonides*

Sulphurs (Subfamily Coliadinae)
❏ Clouded Sulphur   *Colias philodice*
❏ Orange Sulphur   *Colias eurytheme*
❏ Pink-edged Sulphur   *Colias interior*

Gossamer-Wings (Family Lycaenidae)
Harvesters (Subfamily Miletinae)
❏ Harvester   *Feniseca tarquinius*

Coppers (Subfamily Lycaeninae)
❏ American Copper   *Lycaena phlaeas*
❏ Bronze Copper   *Lycaena hyllus*
❏ Bog Copper   *Lycaena epixanthe*
❏ Dorcas Copper   *Lycaena dorcas*
❏ Purplish Copper   *Lycaena helloides*

Hairstreaks and Elfins (Subfamily Theclinae)
❏ Coral Hairstreak   *Satyrium titus*
❏ Acadian Hairstreak   *Satyrium acadica*
❏ Edwards' Hairstreak   *Satyrium edwardsii*
❏ Banded Hairstreak   *Satyrium calanus*
❏ Hickory Hairstreak   *Satyrium caryaevorum*
❏ Striped Hairstreak   *Satyrium liparops*
❏ Gray Hairstreak   *Strymon melinus*
❏ Brown Elfin   *Callophrys augustinus*
❏ Hoary Elfin   *Callophrys polios*
❏ Henry's Elfin   *Callophrys henrici*
❏ Eastern Pine Elfin   *Callophrys niphon*
❏ Western Pine Elfin   *Callophrys eryphon*

Blues (Subfamily Polyommatinae)
- Eastern Tailed-Blue   *Everes comyntas*
- Western Tailed-Blue   *Everes amyntula*
- Spring Azure   *Celastrina ladon*
- Summer Azure   *Celastrina ladon neglecta*
- Silvery Blue   *Glaucopsyche lygdamus*
- Greenish Blue   *Plebejus saepiolus*
- Karner Melissa Blue   *Lycaeides melissa samuelis*
- Northern Blue   *Lycaeides idas*
- Nabokov's Blue   *Lycaeides idas nabokovi*

Brushfoots (Family Nymphalidae)
Fritillaries (Subfamily Heliconiinae)
- Variegated Fritillary   *Euptoieta claudia*
- Great Spangled Fritillary   *Speyeria cybele*
- Aphrodite Fritillary   *Speyeria aphrodite*
- Atlantis Fritillary   *Speyeria atlantis*
- Arctic Fritillary   *Boloria chariclea*
- Bog Fritillary   *Boloria eunomia*
- Silver-bordered Fritillary   *Boloria selene*
- Meadow Fritillary   *Boloria bellona*
- Frigga Fritillary   *Boloria frigga*
- Freija Fritillary   *Boloria freija*

Checkerspots, Crescents and Anglewings (Subfamily Nymphalinae)
- Gorgone Checkerspot   *Chlosyne gorgone*
- Silvery Checkerspot   *Chlosyne nycteis*
- Harris' Checkerspot   *Chlosyne harrisii*
- Baltimore Checkerspot   *Euphydryas phaeton*
- Pearl Crescent   *Phyciodes tharos*
- Northern Crescent   *Phyciodes selenis*
- Tawny Crescent   *Phyciodes batesii*
- Question Mark   *Polygonia interrogationis*
- Eastern Comma   *Polygonia comma*
- Satyr Comma   *Polygonia satyrus*
- Green Comma   *Polygonia faunus*
- Gray Comma   *Polygonia progne*
- Hoary Comma   *Polygonia gracilis*
- Compton Tortoiseshell   *Nymphalis vaualbum*
- Milbert's Tortoiseshell   *Nymphalis milberti*
- Mourning Cloak   *Nymphalis antiopa*
- American Lady   *Vanessa virginiensis*
- Painted Lady   *Vanessa cardui*
- Red Admiral   *Vanessa atalanta*

Admirals and Viceroy (Subfamily Limenitidinae)
- White Admiral   *Limenitis arthemis arthemis*
- Red-spotted Purple   *Limenitis arthemis astyanax*
- Viceroy   *Limenitis archippus*

Satyrs and Wood-Nymphs (Subfamily Satyrinae)
❏ Northern Pearly-eye   *Enodia anthedon*
❏ Eyed Brown   *Satyrodes eurydice*
❏ Appalachian Brown   *Satyrodes appalachia*
❏ Little Wood-Satyr   *Megisto cymela*
❏ Common Ringlet   *Coenonympha tullia*
❏ Common Wood-Nymph   *Cercyonis pegala*
❏ Red-disked Alpine   *Erebia discoidalis*
❏ Disa Alpine   *Erebia disa mancinus*
❏ Macoun's Arctic   *Oeneis macounii*
❏ Chryxus Arctic   *Oeneis chryxus*
❏ Jutta Arctic   *Oeneis jutta*

Monarchs (Subfamily Danainae)
❏ Monarch   *Danaus plexippus*

Skippers (Family Hesperidae)
Spread-winged Skippers (Subfamily Pyrginae)
❏ Silver-spotted Skipper   *Epargyreus clarus*
❏ Northern Cloudywing   *Thorybes pylades*
❏ Dreamy Duskywing   *Erynnis icelus*
❏ Sleepy Duskywing   *Erynnis brizo*
❏ Juvenal's Duskywing   *Erynnis juvenalis*
❏ Mottled Duskywing   *Erynnis martialis*
❏ Columbine Duskywing   *Erynnis lucilius*
❏ Wild Indigo Duskywing   *Erynnis baptisiae*

Grass Skippers (Subfamily Hesperiinae)
❏ Arctic Skipper   *Carterocephalus palaemon*
❏ Least Skipper   *Ancyloxypha numitor*
❏ European Skipper   *Thymelicus lineola*
❏ Common Branded Skipper   *Hesperia comma*
❏ Leonard's Skipper   *Hesperia leonardus*
❏ Cobweb Skipper   *Hesperia metea*
❏ Indian Skipper   *Hesperia sassacus*
❏ Peck's Skipper   *Polites peckius*
❏ Tawny-edged Skipper   *Polites themistocles*
❏ Crossline Skipper   *Polites origenes*
❏ Long Dash   *Polites mystic*
❏ Northern Broken-Dash   *Wallengrenia egeremet*
❏ Little Glassywing   *Pompeius verna*
❏ Delaware Skipper   *Atrytone logan*
❏ Hobomok Skipper   *Poanes hobomok*
❏ Broad-winged Skipper   *Poanes viator*
❏ Dion Skipper   *Euphyes dion*
❏ Black Dash   *Euphyes conspicua*
❏ Two-spotted Skipper   *Euphyes bimacula*
❏ Dun Skipper   *Euphyes vestris*
❏ Dusted Skipper   *Atrytonopsis hianna*
❏ Pepper and Salt Skipper   *Amblyscirtes hegon*
❏ Common Roadside-Skipper   *Amblyscirtes vialis*

Appendix B
Habitat Guide

Bogs

Pink-edged Sulphur
Bronze Copper
Bog Copper
Dorcas Copper
Spring Azure
Silvery Blue
Aphrodite Fritillary
Atlantis Fritillary
Bog Fritillary
Silver-bordered Fritillary
Meadow Fritillary
Harris' Checkerspot
Baltimore Checkerspot
Common Ringlet
Jutta Arctic
Arctic Skipper
Dreamy Duskywing
Black Dash

Swamps

Spring Azure
Eastern Comma
Gray Comma
Milbert's Tortoiseshell
Mourning Cloak
Viceroy
Northern Pearly-eye
Eyed Brown
Arctic Skipper
Pepper and Salt Skipper

Sandy Areas

Silvery Blue
Silvery Checkerspot
Sleepy Duskywing

Deciduous Forests

Canadian Tiger Swallowtail
Mustard White
Spring Azure
Aphrodite Fritillary
Atlantis Fritillary
Gray Comma
Compton Tortoiseshell
Northern Pearly-eye
Little Wood-Satyr
Silver-spotted Skipper
Dreamy Duskywing
Sleepy Duskywing
Juvenal's Duskywing

Coniferous Forests

White Admiral
Green Comma
Arctic Skipper

Oak Woodlands

Pink-edged Sulphur
Edwards' Hairstreak
Banded Hairstreak
Aphrodite Fritillary
Baltimore Checkerspot
Sleepy Duskywing
Juvenal's Duskywing
Arctic Skipper

Burned Areas

Pink-edged Sulphur (wherever
blueberry plants are found.)
Silvery Blue
Silvery Checkerspot

Appendix C
Phenology Flight Chart

Pg.	Species	March	April	May
94	Mourning Cloak	▓	▓	▓
90	Compton Tortoiseshell	▓	▓	▓
84	Eastern Comma	▓	▓	▓
88	Gray Comma	▓	▓	▓
92	Milbert's Tortoiseshell	▓	▓	▓
82	Question Mark		▓	▓
54	Spring Azure		▓	▓
126	Dreamy Duskywing			▓
28	Clouded Sulphur			▓
26	Cabbage White			▓
20	Cdn Tiger Swallowtail			▓
36	American Copper			▓
96	American Lady			▓
98	Painted Lady			▓
52	Eastern Tailed-Blue			▓
72	Meadow Fritillary			▓
18	Black Swallowtail			▓
100	Red Admiral			▓
30	Orange Sulphur			▓
102	White Admiral			▓
118	Monarch			▓
106	Northern Pearly-eye			
32	Pink-edged Sulphur			
76	Harris' Checkerspot			
132	European Skipper			
62	Great Spangled Fritillary			
46	Coral Hairstreak			
114	Common Wood-Nymph			
64	Aphrodite Fritillary			
108	Eyed Brown			
104	Viceroy			
40	Bog Copper			

June	July	August	September	October

Appendix D
Favorite Food List

Alfalfa
Medicago sativa

American Elm
Ulmas americana

American Red Raspberry
Rubus strigosus

Apple
Pyrus malus

Arrowheads
Sagittaria species

Ashes
Fraxinus species

Aspens
Populus species

Asters (above)
Aster species

Barnyard-Grass
Echinochloa crusgalli

Basswood
Tilia americana

Beard-Tongues
Penstemon species

Beggar's-Ticks
Bidens species

Big Bluestem
Andropogon gerardii

Birches
Betula species

Bird's-foot Trefoil
Lotus corniculatus

Black-eyed Susan (above)
Rudbeckia hirta

Black Snakeroot
Sanicula marilandica

Blackberries
Rubus species

Blazing-Stars
Liatris species

Blue Vervain
Verbena hastata

Blueberries (above)
Vaccinium species

Bog Goldenrod
Solidago uliginosa

Bog Laurel (above)
Kalmia polifolia

Bog Rosemary
Andromeda glaucophylla

Boneset
Eupatorium perfoliatum

Brome-Grass
Bromus species

Bur Oak
Quercus macrocarpa

Burdock
Arctium minus

Buttercups
Ranunculus species

Catnip
Nepeta cataria

Cherries
Prunus species

Clover (above)
Trifolium species

Chokecherry
Prunus virginiana

Cinquefoil
Potentilla species

Common Milkweed (above)
Asclepias syriaca

Cotton-Grasses
Eriophorum species

Cottonwood
Populus deltoides

Cow Parsnip
Heracleum lanatum

Crab-Grasses
Digitaria species

Crown Vetch
Coronilla varia

Curly Dock
Rumex crispus

Currants
Ribes species

Dandelion
Taraxacum officinale

Dewberry
Rubus pubescens

Dill
Anethum graveolens

Dogwoods
Cornus species

Dwarf Ginseng
Panax trifolium

Elms
Ulmus species

English Plantain
Plantago lanceolata

Fireweed
Epilobium angustifolium

Flat-topped White Aster
Aster umbellatus

Fleabanes
Erigeron species

Goldenrods (above)
Solidago species

Gooseberries
Ribes species

Hackberry
Celtis occidentalis

Hawthorns
Crataegus species

Hedge Nettles
Stachys species

Hoary Puccoon
Lithospermum canascens

Hog Peanut
Amphicarpaea bracteata

Honeysuckles
Diervilla & Lonicera species

Hops
Humulus lupulus

Kentucky Blue Grass
Poa pratensis

Knotweeds
Polygonum species

Labrador Tea (above)
Ledum groenlandicum

Large-fruited Cranberry
Vaccinium macrocarpum

Late Sweet Blueberry
Vaccinium angustifolium

Lilac
Syringa vulgaris

Lupines
Lupinus species

Marsh Cinquefoil
Potentilla palustris

Meadowsweet
Spirea alba

Milk-Vetches
Astragalus species

Mints
Labiatae family

Mustards
Cruciferae family

Nettle
Urtica dioica

New Jersey Tea
Ceanothus americanus

Northern Red Oak
Quercus rubra

Northern White Violet
Viola pallens

Orange Hawkweed (above)
Hieracium aurantiacum

Orchard Grass
Dactylus glomerata

Ox-eye Daisy (above)
Chrysanthemum leucanthemum

Panic Grasses
Panicum species

Paper Birch
Betula papyrifera

Parsnip
Pastinaca sativa

Pearly Everlasting
Anaphalis margaritacea

Peppergrass
Lepidium densiflorum

Purple Loosestrife
Lythrum salicaria

Purple Reed Grass
Calamagrostis purpurascens

Pussy Toes
Antennaria species

Quack-Grass
Agropyron repens

Radishes
Raphanus sativus

Ragworts
Senecio species

Red Clover
Trifolium pratense

Red Fescue
Festuca rubra

Red-berried Elder
Sambucus pubens

Rock Cresses
Arabis species

Sandbar Willow
Salix exigua

Sarsaparillas
Aralia species

Satin-Grasses
Muhlenbergia species

Self-Heal
Prunella vulgaris

Sheep Sorrel
Rumex acetosella

Shorthusk Grasses
Brachyelytrum species

Shrubby Cinquefoil
Potentilla fruticosa

Small Blue Aster
Aster simplex

Speckled Alder
Alnus rugosa

Spotted Joe-Pye Weed
(above)
Eupatorium maculatum

Spotted Knapweed (above)
Centaurea biebersteinii

Spreading Dogbane (below)
Apocynum androsaemifolium

Staghorn Sumac
Rhus typhina

Swamp Milkweed
Asclepias incarnata

Sweet Cicelies
Osmorhiza species

Thistles (above)
Cirsium & *Sonchus* species

Timothy
Phleum pratense

Turtlehead
Chelone glabra

Vetches
Astragalus & *Vicia* species

Viburnums
Viburnum species

Violets
Viola species

Virgin's Bower
Clematis virginiana

Virginia Waterleaf
Hydrophyllum virginianum

Water Dock
Rumex orbiculata

Water Hemlocks
Cicuta species

Water Parsnip
Sium suave

White Clover
Trifolium repens

White Sweetclover
Melilotus alba

White-Grasses
Leersia species

Wild Bergamot
Monarda fistulosa

Wild Iris (above)
Iris versicolor

Wild Mint
Mentha arvensis

Wild Peas
Lathyrus species

Wild Plum
Prunus americana &
P. nigra

Wild Roses
Rosa species

Wild Strawberries
Fragaria species

Willows
Salix species

Winter-Cresses
Barbarea species

Wood Lily
Lilium philadelphicum

Wood Nettle
Laportea canadensis

Wooly Blue Violet
Viola sororia

Wormwoods
Artemisia species

Yarrow
Achillea millefolium

Yellow Hawkweed
Hieracium species

Yellow Sweetclover
Melilotus officinalis

Appendix E
Titles of Interest

Glassberg, J. 1999. *Butterflies through Binoculars: The East*. New York: Oxford University Press.

Holmes, A.M. et.al. 1991. *The Ontario Butterfly Atlas*. Toronto Entomologists' Association.

Klassen, P., Westwood, A.R., Preston, W.B. and McKillop, W.B. 1989. *The Butterflies of Manitoba*. Winnipeg, Manitoba: Museum of Man and Nature.

Layberry, R.A., Hall, P.W., and Lafontaine J.D. 1998. *The Butterflies of Canada*. Toronto, Ontario: University of Toronto Press.

Nielsen, M.C. 1999. *Michigan Butterflies and Skippers*. East Lansing, MI: Michigan State University, Extension Bulletin E-2675.

Opler, P.A. 1994. *Peterson First Guide to Butterflies and Moths*. New York, NY: Houghton-Mifflin.

Opler, P.A. 1992. *A Field Guide to Eastern Butterflies*. New York, NY: Houghton-Mifflin.

Opler, P.A. and Krizek, G.O. 1984. *Butterflies East of the Great Plains*. Baltimore, MD: Johns Hopkins University Press.

Pyle, R.M. 1984, 1992. *Handbook for Butterfly Watchers*. New York, NY: Houghton-Mifflin.

Pyle, R.M. 1981. *The Audubon Society Field Guide to North American Butterflies*. New York, NY: Alfred A. Knopf.

Scott, J.A. 1986. *The Butterflies of North America*. Stanford, CA: Stanford University Press.

Shaw, J. 1987. *John Shaw's Closeups in Nature*. New York, NY: Amphoto.

Swengel, A.B. 1995. *Checklist of the Butterflies of Northwestern Wisconsin*. Madison, WI: Madison Audubon Society.

Walton, R.K. 1990. *The Audubon Society Pocket Guides: Familiar Butterflies of North America*. New York, NY: Knopf.

Weber, L. 1996. *Backyard Almanac*. Duluth, MN: Pfeifer-Hamilton Publishers.

West, L. and Ridl J. 1994. *How to Photograph Insects and Spiders*. Mechanicsburg, PA: Stackpole Books.

Wright, A.B. 1993. *Peterson First Guide to Caterpillars of North America*. New York, NY: Houghton-Mifflin.

Appendix F
Binoculars for Butterflying

Better, close-focusing optics have opened the door to the hobby of butterflying. Close-focusing is a must, full-size is preferable and power is a matter of choice. Listed here is a sampling of the best binoculars for watching our winged jewels.

Weight is listed because some folks prefer lighter optics. The compacts are lighter, but they also gather less light at dawn and dusk. They are also harder to hold steady than their full-size cousins. Compact binoculars are nice for easy packing.

Good butterflying binoculars should focus under ten feet. This gives you the magnification you need for the butterfly to fill your field-of-view.

The last column represents relative brightness. The higher the number the brighter your view will be. This is important for picking out details at dawn and dusk. Brightness is not the big deal it is with birding binoculars. Most butterflying will be done in the middle of the day when the butterflies are active. Birds on the other hand, are active at dusk and dawn and so bright binoculars are a must.

What is the difference between 10-power and 8-power? With increased power one loses brightness. As stated above, this may not be a big problem with butterflying. Also with higher power binoculars any body movement is magnified.

Brand	size	weight (in oz.)	closest focus	brightness
Bausch & Lomb				
8x42 WP Elite	full-size	29	5	28
10x42 WP Elite	full-size	28	5	18
7x26 Custom	compact	13	6	14
9x26 Custom	compact	13	8	8
10x42 WP Discoverer	full-size	30	8	18
8x24 Legacy	compact	8	8	9
Bushnell				
8x42 Legend	full-size	30	6	28
10x42 Legend	full-size	30	6	18
Canon				
5x17 FC	compact	7	5	12
7x17 FC	compact	7	5	6

Brand	size	weight (in oz.)	closest focus	brightness
Celestron				
8x42 Regal	full-size	23	6	28
10x42 Regal	full-size	28	8	25
Kahles				
8x42 DCF	full-size	26	8	28
10x42 DCF	full-size	26	8	18
Leica				
8x20 BC/BCA Pocket	compact	8	9	6
8x32 BA Ultra	full-size	22	7	16
10x32 BA Ultra	full-size	22	7	10
Minolta				
8x25 Activa	compact	10	8	10
10x25 Activa	compact	10	8	6
Nikon				
8x42 Venturer LX	full-size	35	9	28
10x42 Venturer LX	full-size	35	9	18
Pentax				
8x32 DCF WP	full-size	21	8	16
8x42 DCF WP	full-size	26	8	28
10x42 DCF WP	full-size	26	8	18
10x25 DCF MC	compact	11	7	6
Swarovski				
8x20 B-P	compact	8	7	6
8.5x42 EL	full-size	29	8	24
10x42 EL	full-size	28	8	18
Swift				
7x36 Eaglet WP	full-size	21	5	26
10x42 Viceroy WP	full-size	24	6	18
Zeiss				
8x30 Classic	full-size	21	9	14
10x40 Victory	full-size	26	8	16

Appendix G
Butterfly Conservation Groups and Websites

North American Butterfly Association (NABA)
4 Delaware Road
Morristown, NJ 07960
www.naba.org

Lepidopterists' Society
1608 Presidio Way
Roseville, CA 95661
www.furman.edu

Xerces Society
4828 Southeast Hawthorne Boulevard
Portland, OR 97215
www.xerces.org

The Nature Conservancy
1815 Lynn Street
Arlington, VA 22209
www.tnc.org

Appendix H
Photographic Credits

All photographs in this book, except the ones listed below, were taken by the author.

Jeffrey Glassberg: pages 44, 65, 75, 96, 108, 127, 129, 140, 142.

Rod Planck: pages 7 (top), 18, 19, 21 (top), 25 (bottom), 40, 77, 79, 82, 119 (bottom).

Sparky Stensaas: pages 3 (top), 21 (bottom), 27 (bottom), 33, 162 (all), 163 (all), 164 (all).

Ann Swengel: pages 29, 42, 43 (top and bottom), 64, 68, 69, 71, 116, 117, 135, 137, 149.

Index

Field Notes

Field Notes

Field Notes

Field Notes